Child of a Child

A Story of Trial, Trauma And Triumph

By

DR. MONICA SANCHEZ

ISBN: 979-8-86-134528-6

I dedicate this book to the loving memory of my beloved grandparents, William and Virginia Subryan (the Queen), and my mother, Ena Subryan. I also dedicate it to my children, Paul Anthony Halley, Monica Dawn Sanchez, and Howard Silk Runcie, and to all my grandchildren and great-grandchildren.

Contents

Foreword

"We are unlimited beings; limited only by the concept of
limitation that we hold in our minds." - Lester Levenson

I feel totally honored and sincerely privileged to have been singled out by
the author to write the *Foreword* to this singularly commendable exercise in
outstanding literary effort. This book is not only timely, but is also apt for a
season in which, although the world, with each passing day, appears to be
seemingly immune to the plight of people who are existing on the fringes of
material sustenance and wellbeing, we are fortunate to still have men and
women of conscience across the divides of the world's different convictions
and persuasions who are totally committed to upholding human dignity to
the highest possible standards, and contributing their own noble quota to
peace on our planet. Monica Sanchez is one such individual.

Even more remarkably, at no time in the history of mankind has there
been so many opportunities to continue to advance the cause of human
wellbeing on all conceivable fronts, be it economic or social. For all practical
purposes, that also means the time is propitious for all of us to sincerely
commit to championing the causes so eloquently promoted by the United
Nations Sustainable Development Goals 2030, especially in the areas of
poverty alleviation, gender equality, food security and the preservation and
protection of the girl child.

That is also why, for me, it has been a totally humbling experience reading the story of the author, a truly remarkable woman who I met for the first time in January of 2003. Since then I have remained an integral part of the story of someone whom I hold in the highest esteem, not only because she is one of those women who are deploying valiant effort to making the world a kinder and fairer place through their industry, courage, compassion and indomitability of spirit, but also because of her resolute and resilient commitment to those ideals that she holds sacrosanct. That Ms Sanchez, an accomplished woman of many exemplary parts, committed human rights advocate, and global humanitarian, possesses the unassailable credentials that equip her to authoritatively write a book of this nature is quite beyond a shadow of the slightest doubt, and I endorse her brilliant effort with every fiber of my being.

Today, as I write the *Foreword* to this captivating memoir, I share who Monica Sanchez is, and all that God has designed her to be. *Child of A Child* truly speaks into her entire journey, and all that it took for her to get to where she is today. Suffice it to say that God is definitely not through with her yet. There are many real life experiences she had to pass through, including betrayal, failed relationships, hatred, domestic violence, and so much more. Monica's life, as she relates it in this remarkable book, is authentic. It is raw. It is unfiltered. She has lived, and is still living her life above the toxic narrative, while courageously forging ahead with her life mission. She has had to be uncommonly strong amidst daunting setbacks, obstacles, defeat, persecution, and betrayal. Yet, she remains standing!

As you read, and as you proceed on this journey with Monica, allow yourself to feel, to wonder, to laugh, to cry, and to just *be*. There is so much that she unpacks, and I think it is just beautiful that you have allowed yourself to gain access to all that she shares from the depth of her soul. As you read her story, you will realize that God is bigger than her journey, and *your* own journey, for that matter. More importantly, you will feel yourself becoming empowered to never give up, but to keep going, no matter what gets in your way.

To Monica herself, I have these heartfelt words to say:

Despite what was, this is your now;
No longer in chains, no longer bound.
The trials of life came to make you stronger.
Hold your head high up, because you are a survivor;
You are a conqueror.

You struggled to break the chains of abuse and rejection.
Although you were betrayed and tormented;
By those who were meant to protect and love you;
You insisted on remaining the Queen that you are,
You loved being who you were;
And, deep down inside;
You needed a new direction;
To break free of abuse,
And the chain of torment.

Monica, no longer do you have to wear a mask;
Or put on a façade.
You might have been mistreated by family,
Ridiculed, betrayed and lied upon.
But, you were always accepted by God.
You are a woman;
Child of a child,
But, more importantly, you are a child of the Living God.

Danny Glover
San Francisco, California
United States of America

Acknowledgement

First and foremost, I give God the glory, praise, and gratitude for sustaining me through the years.

I acknowledged my mentor and coach, Dr. Abayomi Garnett, the driving force behind my efforts in achieving the goal of completing the manuscript of this book.

I acknowledge my dear friend and wonderful destiny helper through the years, multiple award-winning Hollywood actor, movie star, and eminent United Nations humanitarian ambassador, Mr. Danny Glover.

I also acknowledge all those other friends who I sincerely consider my family, and who have given me invaluable support throughout this journey.

Finally, I will remain eternally grateful to the United Nations for providing the platform for the full expression of my deepest desires, and the fervent yearnings of my heart to make that significant impact that will make the world a better place for women and girls, and which will make our planet a place where no one remains hungry, ill-educated, and homeless, fundamental human rights not being a privilege, but a birthright.

A Diamond Jubilee Tribute

"Onlookers cannot see behind the mask of perfection,
That behind your trademark smile you are power,
That behind that sweet smile you are wisdom borne of pain,
And strength nurtured by courage.

Monica,
There you stand holding on tightly,
Yet, no one can see,
That hint of light that shines through your eyes,
The eyes of a Caribbean queen.

You drift a little into that abysmal place,
There, the memories of that eight-year-old child,
Filled with the agony of a distant past,
Forgiven but never forgotten.

You stand all dressed in crimson,
Like a diamond shining with a luminescent glow.
You stand in your dream,
You hold others spellbound in that dream,
A dream mined not by imagination but by blood,
Yet, this is not a dream.

You stand smiling, filled with thought,
Thoughts of your journey, and of your own liberation,
WOW!!!

You stand in your light,
The reality is me as a child,
One of the forgotten,
We, the forgotten,
Will never forget what is forgotten,
For, the forgotten never forget,
Today, I come of age as a diamond.
I am a diamond,
A blood diamond,
Mined by blood,
Sculpted by experience,
For a new day of hope,
And a new age of glory."

Antoinette Pitcan, New York, December 23, 2019

Introduction

"From this day forward we shall need the goodwill and hard work of all our people so that we may proceed to make our country a fit and proper home for heroes in the struggle for political and economic independence. Let there be an end to sectional racial quarrels and suspicions so that national unity may be restored."
- Cheddi Jagan, Fourth President of Guyana (1992 - 1997)

Guyana has a rich and totally fascinating history of a long and tumultuous colonial past. Sadly, it is a history that has been marred by it's own people, and its adopted natives. The verdict of history may well be that much of the beautiful country's history has been soiled, first by the race issues created by the colonialists, and secondly by the petty jealousies that each of the major races, the *East Indian* and the *African,* would later display towards each other

Indeed, the two major ethnic groupings in Guyana are the East Indian and the Black. Guyana's motto is *"One People, One Nation, One Destiny."* The tragic irony is that the existence of the country as a nation-state would over the years be nothing but a total contradiction of these principles of unity and indivisibility. Guyana's ethnic constitution is 51% East Indian and 43% AfroGuyanese. Malignant racial conflict and division has detrimentally affected the country socially, economically and politically, and this will, in all likelihood, continue until and unless something more salutary happens to the fragile coexistence of East Indian and African ethnic groups in Guyana.

In gaining a fine understanding of the mechanics of Guyana as a nation, certain facts must be acknowledged. *One,* Guyana was a British colony where Africans were enslaved, and Indians later brought to be indentured to replace them. Necessarily, therefore, after some decades, the Indian and African evolved to become the two major ethnic groupings in the country. *Two*, a high index of conflict would later arise between these two major ethnic groups, resulting in the organization of their political system along very rigid ethnic lines. *Three,* it was the need for cheap labor that landed both groups, Indian and African, by chance in the Caribbean. Africans were brought to Guyana and enslaved on sugar and cotton plantations from the 17th century until the early 19th century, when the slave trade was abolished in 1833. *Four,* East Indians were later imported into the colony as indentured laborers to replace the liberated Africans on the plantations. Racial stereotypes quickly developed in the colony. For instance, British plantation owners characterized Africans as physically strong but lazy and irresponsible. On the other hand, the East Indians were stereotyped as industrious but clannish and greedy. It is instructive that these stereotypical views are still prevalent to this day. To feel sleepy after eating is referred to in Guyana, and perhaps most of the Caribbean countries, as having *"niggeritis,"* a direct and not-too-subtle allusion to the laziness of Africans. To a considerable extent, these stereotypes were accepted as valid by the immigrant groups themselves, with each, not surprisingly, conveniently validating the positive stereotypes of itself and conferring the negative stereotypes on the other group. Put differently, they believed what was said of the other group but none of what was said of them. These stereotypes would later provide a foundation for both behavioral characteristics, and easily justifiable competition among the groups. Africans were described as indolent when they refused to work for low wages or enter into long-term contracts with the plantations as the Indians had. East Indians were considered selfish when they minimized their expenses to accumulate wealth.

In modern day Guyana, the association of behavior with ethnicity is less rigid than it was in the colonial era. Where once, there was a sharp and uniform distinction between behavior considered *'British'* and behavior considered '*coolie,*' these days there is a range of situations that can receive different ethnic colorations in different situations. For instance, acting 'coolie' in a situation could be something as simple as wearing a dress ensemble with uncoordinated or unmatched colors. Demonstrating 'British' behavior would be an insistence on speaking the Queen's English instead of the local Creole. What is considered 'British' in a rural village might be considered 'coolie' in the towns. In addition to stereotyping, a colonial value system that favored European beliefs, specifically British ideals, has been encouraged. Euro-centric beliefs were promoted by the colonial education system, which, naturally, idealized British customs. The former slaves, perceiving their Christianity to be incontrovertible proof that they were as civilized as the British, accepted the superiority of British culture.

Since the late 19th century, the emerging middle class of urban AfroGuyanese and Indo-Guyanese have inevitably developed a nationalist ideology based largely on British values, and they have claimed their elitist place in society because they have largely met standards that had been set by the British. Ethnic perception among these separate groups has emerged from the divisions of color, religion, place of residence, and occupation. Later, the policies of ethnic rule changed from politics based on *ethnic preference* to politics based on *ethnic dominance*. Both groups became envious of each other's successes. There existed a high degree of racial exclusivity in residential concentration of the population in the villages and townships, which emphasized economic separation. Simply put, the two groups hardly mingled. Communities were either solely African or solely Indian, and it was only in the more urban areas that there were more integrated communities. This lack of racial integration remains to this day.

The 1957 elections in Guyana, held under a new constitution, gave credence to the growing ethnic division within the Guyanese electorate. The People's Progressive Party (PPP) had two wings. One was headed by Linden Forbes Sampson Burnham, while the the other was led by Cheddi Jagan. The 1957 elections were won by Jagan's PPP faction. The party's main supporters were increasingly identified as Indo-Guyanese, and this led to more rice land, improved union representation in the sugar industry, improved business opportunities and more and better government jobs for the Indo-Guyanese. The PPP soon ceased from being a multiracial party, becoming a solely Indo-Guyanese party. Another significant factor was soon added to the developing tension. Burnham would never forget the lessons he learned from the 1957 elections. He knew he could not win the elections with support only from the lower class, urban Afro-Guyanese. He needed middle-class allies, especially those AfroGuyanese who backed the moderate United Democratic Party (a party sympathetic to Jagan). Burnham began to work to create a balance between maintaining the support of the more radical Afro-Guyanese lower classes and gaining the support of the more capitalist middle class. He would now need a common uniting force to keep these two groups together and himself in power. The answer was really quite simple: manipulate racial sentiment. However, this solution would prove to be not only simple but disastrous. Burnham's appeals to race proved highly successful in bridging the rift that divided the Afro-Guyanese along class lines. This strategy convinced the powerful Afro-Guyanese middle class to accept a leader who was more of a radical than they would have preferred to support. Burnham's and Jagan's conflicting economic policy views led to their split in the PPP. Burnham snatched the United Democratic Party from under Jagan's feet and broke away from the PPP altogether to form the People's National Congress (PNC).

Burnham was a socialist. He saw the immediate goal to be the attainment of political independence after which the country would sustain itself by producing everything it would need. Jagan, on the other hand was a Marxist. He saw economic exploitation as the main problem. This set Jagan on a collision course with the United States, and he lost his position as leader. British troops landed in Guyana, suspended the constitution, and threw the PPP out of office. This would later prove to be a mere smokescreen. What wasn't immediately obvious was that the United States was sponsoring a covert operation. The United States had supported this intervention.

Most Guyanese were not aware that what was taking place was a major anti-communist offensive by the United States in Guyana. After this, Jagan strengthened his hold on the Indo-Guyanese Community. Though he openly expressed his admiration for Josef Stalin, Mao Zedong, and, later Fidel Castro, Jagan felt that his Marxist ideals could be applied uniquely to Guyana. Interestingly, in the late 1950s, the British Caribbean colonies had been actively negotiating the establishment of a West Indies Federation. There was a growing agreement among non-Indian politicians that federation with the rest of the British West Indies offered the best post-colonial political solution for the colonies. The issue, however, inflamed the passions of the East Indian population and its political representatives who were already worried of the possibility of black political domination. The Indo-Guyanese were apprehensive of becoming part of a federation in which they felt people of African descent would outnumber them, and that it was a plot to deprive them of their electoral majority. East Indian leaders were strong in the belief that it's ratification would have had the effect of decreasing the East Indian population to an insignificant minority by initiating mass migration of Africans into the colony from other lesser developed West Indian countries. East Indians felt that "Indians had worked to build the country, and blacks wanted to get the better of Indians." The East Indian population was led by its leaders to believe that a West Indian federation would erase any possibility Indians had of any representation in future governments. Jagan was the chief voice of East Indian opposition to the Federation in Guyana. By contrast Burnham, the Afro-Guyanese leader, fully supported the federation. Jagan's veto of the federation caused his party to lose all significant Afro-Guyanese support.

In the early 1900's, Marcus Garvey and other black intellectuals began to preach *"Africa for Africans,"* which spurred a great resurgence in Afro-centricity and black pride, deepening the divide between Indian and black. Almost simultaneously, there was a resurgence in regaining ties with India. Indo-Guyanese women began wearing Indian garb. These factors all compounded to widen the gulf between these two races. Clearly, The Black

Power Movement was viewed with extreme suspicion by the Indo-Guyanese since it totally failed to provide the necessary groundwork within the Indian community. The term "black" moreover, generally referred to persons of predominantly African descent. Most Indians did not regard themselves as being black. To underscore this point, an Indian writer responded negatively to having been categorized as such by the Black Power Movement. He wrote: *"I object to being black. Indians belong to the Caucasian or "white" race. Why then call Indians black? You the Black Power members are asking us to join you in your march for power. Your sudden interest in the East Indian sugar worker is viewed with suspicion. We are not prepared to support you."* This clearly showed that Black Power, or even Indian Power for that matter, has no place in Guyana, because, although it advances both peoples, it ignores the existence of each other. In all probability, it is a concept that will only destroy the slow integration process that is anxiously anticipated by well-meaning members of both groups.

Since independence in 1963, two characteristics have dominated Guyanese society and politics; the presence of strong political personalities like Cheddi Jagan, Linden Forbes Sampson Burnham and Desmond Hoyte, and ethno-racial divisions based on mutual suspicion and manipulation by these strong personalities. At the same time, the struggle for political ascendancy between Burnham, the hero of the Afro-Guyanese, and Jagan, the hero of the Indo-Guyanese masses, left a legacy of racially-polarized politics that remained in place in the 1990's. The race politics practiced in Guyana, where political majoritism aligned one group against another was extremely harmful to the country. The result of the enactment policy in Guyana almost resulted in civil war, where blacks burnt the businesses of Indo-Guyanese, and during the ensuing melee, hundreds of Africans and East Indians lost their lives. There was was an increase in racial tensions, characterized by the looting and ransacking of homes and businesses by both sides. Guyana was almost propelled into Civil War.

Ethnic conflicts have been increasing in recent years, and have tended to increase as greater contact and communication is made between the two groups. Socially, taboos regarding intermarrying led to the preferences for straight hair versus what is considered "nappy" hair. The cultural development of the East Indian population in Guyana has taken on a character that is quite distinctive. Unlike the other racial group, East Indians have remained attached to their religions of Hinduism and Islam, and to the broader cultural tendencies associated with these religions.

However, some changes are becoming manifestly obvious. The traditional caste relationship among the East Indians has lost most of its religious limitations. Money, position and education are the new cultural values which the East Indians now use for social ranking within their ethnic group. Marriage does not often take place between the East Indian and other groups, not so much on account of that group's status, but because of the persistence of marriage patterns brought over from India. Guyana now has an upper class of big businessmen and large planters; an upper middle class of professionals, who are owners of medium-sized businesses, college-level educators, corporate managers, and senior bureaucrats in the public sector, and leaders of voluntary organizations; a lower middle class of small businessmen, primary and secondary school teachers, white collar workers (in private business, in civil administration, and in the parastatals), skilled workers, and owners of medium sized farms; a rural lower class of small peasants, agricultural laborers, seasonal and short-term migrant laborers and the rural unemployed; and finally, a lower class of unskilled and semi-skilled urban laborers and the substantial number of urban unemployed.

Guyana is small in size and population, and so her economy is mostly based on exports, producing only a small amount of products. This results in a limitation on the efforts of economic control. What makes Guyana differ from the more industrialized nations? The answer to this question explains much of Guyana's current economic woes. All countries, small and big, are subject to the effects of outside economic fluctuations. The difference is that the larger, and more industrialized countries have the ability to manage or attempt to manage any economic fluctuations. A small country like Guyana is dependent on limited exports, mostly agricultural and other small products. In Guyana, the existence of race-based politics and poor economic policies led to the breakdown of her economic system. Guyana is ranked just after Haiti on the list of the poorest countries in the Caribbean, with high levels of unemployment, and double-digit inflation, as a result of which the masses suffer unbearably. This is a reason for the mass exodus of immigrants from Guyana to the United States and Europe. Again, one factor affects the other, as this has led to the lack of manpower and brainpower to facilitate any kind of resurgence in the economy of Guyana.

In Guyana, there remains a great fear of cultural domination, with each group wanting to assert the benefits of their own culture. When public figures and public policy attempt to shape the national identity, the response is usually based on *who will control who,* and who the nation will belong to. While the historical struggle for political power is seen as the primary cause for the poor race relations, another cause should be examined. This is an inadequacy in economic resources, leading to the eternal conflict over whom has everything and who doesn't have anything. It would seem that if the economy of Guyana could be rejuvenated, such that enough resources could be available to the satisfaction of all groups, without favoring one group over the other, the ethnic conflict could possibly be improved. Groups should be left to intermingle and develop their own solutions to their own problems. Although the cultural structure of the Indian and African people might appear to belong to distinct compartments, there are more common values shared between the two than appears at first sight. For instance, both appear to accept the British social system and most of its values, although, sadly they accept it as being superior to their own national cultural values. Ironically, nearly all the leaders of Guyana came to power on platforms of social justice and condemnation of any form of racial discrimination.

It is against the background of these socio-political upheavals in the nascent history of my country, Guyana, that I relate the very poignant story that you are about to read. It is a story whose early beginnings were irrevocably shaped by the racially-divided society that Guyana was, and it is a story that totally defined the choices, personal and inadvertent, that I was compelled to make in later years. Finally, it is a story that forms the bedrock of my perception of what my ultimate role will be in the continued evolution of my country among the comity of nations in the Caribbean, and the world at large.

Monica Sanchez
Queens, New York
September 2023

1

A Christmas Child

I was born a little country girl. The date was December 23, 1959, and it was a day that would always highlight my remarkable entrance into this world by virtue of its striking similarity to that of Jesus Christ. As the Holy Book relates it, when Jesus was born, three wise men from the eastern reaches of the ancient empire expended two days of a grueling journey on camels laden with rare goods that they intended to present as gifts to the newborn messiah. They finally traced him to Bethlehem on the day that is now famously and globally known as Christmas Day, the 25th day of December. Therefore, to all intents and purposes, since those wise men started out on their journey on what may easily have been the 23rd day of December, I share the season of birth with our Lord and Savior. In other words, I am a Christmas child.

I am, indeed, a Christmas child. Maybe that is why Christmas, amidst the poignant elements of the story of my life, has come to mean so much to me. Even more significant, I seem to have taken the beauty of childhood Christmas and somehow transformed it into the sheer wonder of adulthood

Christmas. I often wonder whether Christmas was not specially created for me, given the exhilaration of spirit that totally overwhelms me as soon as the Christmas season approaches. Not unnaturally, the fact that I'm also celebrating my birthday in the same season, barely two days to Christmas Day itself, only serves to add to my feelings of unadulterated joy. Yet, even in the the busyness and chaos of Santa Claus and his Christmas gifts, and the Christmas outfits and Christmas trees that adorn our bodies and homes, I never fail to take a moment to appreciate the true meaning of Christmas. I realize that Christmas will mean different things to different people. For me, it is a rare privilege to have my birthday fall in that wonderful period of the year. Yet, I am also profoundly appreciative of the fact that it is a holiday. Christmas also has deep religious significance for me. While for most, Christmas means genuine togetherness, it always saddens me that for some, it can be a period of acute loneliness.

For me, in addition to gift-giving, Christmas is a wonderful occasion to connect to the "true spirit" of Christmas. It is about communion, togetherness, forgiveness, a new start and the magic of remembering what is really important. I attempt to never forget that the true meaning of Christmas is to remember the birth of Christ. It is also a reminder that our true nature, being one of peace, and of harmony, we need to practice goodwill to all men, not only at Christmas, but throughout the entire year. Christmas signifies that we are all connected, and even if we are not physically with someone, we are not alone. We are in fact, all part of one big family; the family of humanity, with all its imperfections, and all its incredible beauty.

Christmas should inspire us to be charitable. It should compel us to reach out and be involved with the community, and lending a helping hand wherever we can. The giving of gifts is wonderful to make someone else happy, while giving us the added benefit of being happy ourselves, as we unavoidably share in their joy. I have found that another way to give is to offer people my full and genuine attention by being fully present for them. The Christmas season is often one in which others need to be listened to with compassion and empathy, while seeing the best in them, and this is because the gift of love and support is one of the most generous gifts we can ever give.

Christmas is a time to be in the company of the people we love, whether they are members of our immediate family, extended family, friends, or even entire strangers that we are just becoming familiar with. Yet, the true meaning of Christmas can extend to our global family. Often, it can mean inviting someone who is lonely over for Christmas dinner. I believe that sharing love and joy, and connecting with our fellow human beings, no matter who they are, is what the true spirit of Christmas is all about. A beautiful aspect of the season, as I have discovered, is that even family tensions can be resolved in the true spirit of Christmas. Christmas Day is a glorious, peaceful and loving day, and it can be used to bring otherwise estranged people closer.

For me, Christmas is also a time of combined reflection and rebirth since, as one year is ending, another is beginning. Christmas is always a wonderful opportunity to look back at all the moments I am grateful for, and express sincere gratitude. It is a time for me to reflect upon my challenges of the fading year, the lessons I have learnt, and the ways in which I can do things differently in the coming year. Yet, it is also a time to be proud of all that I accomplished, and to make renewed commitment to do more of the things that seem to be working in my favor. Ultimately, Christmas is a season of love, joy and fun. There are many different types of love; self-love, unconditional love, romantic love, friendly love, familial love. Christmas can be a combination of them all. We all want to be loving and happy. It is so easy to forget, amidst all the stress and chaos of everyday life, that happiness, apart from being our greatest motivation, is actually our true nature. Christmas is inherently a happy, joyous day, if only because it is a celebration of new life.

Yet, Christmas also signifies a rather dark spot in my life. To put it differently, and perhaps more accurately, Christmas holds another, and much less salutary significance for me. The Christmas of 1997 would mark a remarkable turning point for me in my view of life and living. This is the story. As I will have cause to relate in greater detail later in this chapter, I was born to teenage parents. I was the first child of a mother and father who were 12 and 16 years of age respectively. Both of them were barely into their teenage years when they succumbed to the precocious love affair that resulted in my mother's pregnancy. After an intervening period, details of which I will also give later, my mother became pregnant for my father yet again. It was that pregnancy that resulted in the birth of my brother, Trevor Charles, just a little over three years after I was born. When he was born, my mother was barely 15, and my father was 19. As might be expected, and as was the case with me, my mother was totally incapable of giving my infant brother adequate care, especially because he fell terribly ill soon after he was born. At the hospital, a group of Amerindians, a local tribe, undertook to care for the baby, and so she handed him over to them to raise in their locality of Linden, Mckenzie, where my father's people were also domiciled. At that time, I was with my maternal grandparents on the diametric opposite of the country, in the town of Berbice. That meant my brother and I never knew each other as we were growing up. However, the Amerindians who were raising him took the trouble to introduce him to my father's people, since they lived in the same town. That meant my brother became acquainted with our father and his people long before I even knew who my father was. In fact, I was not to even remotely know I had a brother, and had no relationship with him, until I was about 10 years old. In effect, we were not close. By the time I would meet my father and his people, my life was a living nightmare, and shortly after that I would become practically homeless, and having to vacate that locality only created further distance between my brother and I.

I only returned on a visit to Linden, Mackenzie, many years later, after my son was born. I recall that it was during that visit that a young man came to visit my father, and in the course of their discussion, it became obvious that this young man was my brother. That, perhaps, would be the closest I ever got to him. A few years later, in 1979, shortly after my daughter was born. I returned to Guyana on another visit, this time in very poor health. Right from the beginning, it was a memorable visit in many respects. I was received very warmly by my father and his relations. In fact, I received a deluge of presents from my father and my grandmother, including clothes and trinkets. I have always loved beautiful jewelry, and came to Guyana with an assortment of my favorite jewelry. Then disaster struck. A female cousin who lived in my father's house stole all my jewelry, and all the presents my father and grandmother had given me. I will never forget how traumatized I was by that incident. Not unnaturally, I was both distraught and distressed. The police were invited, and an extensive hunt was mounted to track down the girl. The search lasted all of seven days, during which time my husband, who was in the military, came to Guyana for the first time, and joined in the search. My brother, Trevor Charles, who also lived in that area, seemingly took the pains to visit at my father's house to enquire if the thieving girl had been apprehended, and how the search was progressing. As matters turned out, she was never found, and the end of one week of searching, with no clues as to her whereabouts, the search was abandoned, and my husband left. Shortly after that, I returned to the United States.

Two years later, I returned to Guyana on another visit. My brother came to the house to both welcome me back, and to sincerely express his regrets that the cousin who stole from me was never found. To my chagrin, however, not long after this, we discovered that my brother, who lived not far away from my father, was accommodating this same girl in his house. Apparently, the girl had, all the while, been hiding in his house, and he was the informant who constantly checked on the status of the search for her, to make sure she remained safe. To give further credence to his act of gross duplicity, as soon as everything had quietened down, he informed her that the coast was clear, and she left the area with all the items she had stolen from me. My shock can only be imagined. As might be expected, I became extremely angry at that totally unwholesome discovery. I couldn't believe my own blood brother could behave towards me in such an unconscionable manner.

When I confronted my brother, and asked him how he could possibly accommodate a lady who had dispossessed me, his own sister, of valuable property, he all but dismissed my accusation in an altogether derisive manner. He actually told me that the girl had been of greater assistance to him than I had ever been. In any case, he further said, he did not really know me, and he did not have a relationship with me, and so he felt compelled to demonstrate greater loyalty to her than to me. To describe my disenchantment with my brother is to do gross injustice to my feelings of combined rage, betrayal and disappointment. I developed very strong feelings of anger and resentment towards him. I detached completely from him. I broke off all contact with, and swore never to have anything to do with him again as long as I lived. I did not speak with him for many years, and by that time, it was already too late to make up for lost time. That, in itself, is another story.

Shortly after I started speaking to my brother again, in an attempt to build a relationship after an unfortunate interregnum of 10 years, sometime in 1997, my brother fell severely ill with malaria fever. Apparently, what ought to have been a mild tropical ailment developed into a complicated and protracted illness. To compound matters, he had hemorrhoids and had to have fairly urgent hemorrhoid surgery, which somehow made his overall case even worse. Someone whose immune system was already severely compromised now found himself literally hovering between life and death as a result of severe systemic incapacitation. Tragically, he did not survive the ordeal as, on Christmas Day of 1997, he succumbed to the complications of his illness, and passed away.

As I already mentioned, my brother's passing in December of 1997 would mark a significant turning point in how I viewed the world. The saddest part of his demise was that I never had the opportunity to forgive him for what I considered the ultimate betrayal. Throughout the period from when I accused him of betraying my trust by cohabiting with a lady who stole from me, and the time of his eventual death, I harbored the most virulent feelings of malignant ill-will, simmering resentment and red-hot anger against my own sibling. His name could not be mentioned close to me without my heart thumping in my chest with suppressed rage. Quite frankly, even I was taken aback at the intensity of my ill-will towards my own brother. No one could talk me out of my inability to forgive him. His death, however, was an anticlimax that shook me to my very core. As it were, our roles were suddenly reversed in our saga of sibling friction. At his death, I was filled with remorse for my unforgiving spirit, and now recognizing my extreme folly for what it was, I sought to make peace with him. Yet, I was filled with a hollow feeling of failure. It was rather too late in the day. My nascent forgiving was nothing but medicine after death. It was all too late, as I simply failed to tell him that I had forgiven him. In the circumstances, I turned against myself, and could not bring myself to forgive myself for my unforgiveness. A new journey had started for me. But, first I had to truly come to terms with why I was unable to forgive my brother while he was alive, and its consequences for me.

My irredeemable anger was at the root of my inability to forgive my brother. Anger is one of the most destructive elements in human nature. As I have come to learn, anger is often the vice of the virtuous. It is often the only dark spot on an otherwise noble person's character. Believe it or not, no form of mortal vice does more to demonize us than anger. It embitters life. Its pernicious propensity for breaking up communities is unmatched. Its malignant potential for destroying the most sacred of relationships, and its absolutely evil proclivity for taking the bloom off childhood, is equally unmatched. Definitely, a predisposition to anger is the most virulent obstacle to proper progress in life. While it is simply not my intention to pontificate that anger is not sometimes justified, my conclusion is that the emotion of anger can seriously and negatively impact us in ways that are at complete variance with our commitments, values and goals. I once heard somewhere that anger is as potently explosive as dynamite. Just like dynamite, anger must be handled with wisdom for it not to precipitate destruction, and without self-control, it is difficult to handle anger, which if allowed to get the best of us will only reveal the worst in us. My anger robbed me of objectivity in my relationship with my brother, and I allowed it to fester into bitterness, which is nothing but a cancer of the soul. That cancer was what was responsible for my inability to forgive him. Ultimately, you can no more grasp a piece of hot coal with the intention of hurling it at someone and not getting your hand burnt, than you can grasp anger, and hold on to it, without getting your soul burnt. Anger, apart from leaving burn scars on your soul, also has the propensity to leave indelible scars on the fabric of your relationships with others. Those scars continued to mar my own relationship with my brother, until he left this world without giving me the opportunity to make needed restitution.

With this realization finally came a decision to start to live my life with a forgiving spirit. I finally discovered that forgiveness is the key to my kingdom of inner peace. However, to arrive at the layer of unforgiveness and peel it off, I had to first successively peel off the layers of anger, sadness and hurt, very much as if I was peeling an onion. For me, the beauty of forgiveness is that it finally set me free from the past, and wonderfully freed up my mind for joyful living. These days, I allow no one to belittle my soul by making me hate them. The regular practice of freely forgiving everyone for everything has transformed me into a calmer, kinder and more compassionate person. Certainly, I am now of the opinion that forgiveness ranks as the greatest spiritual act of love I could ever muster for myself, and for others.

Indeed, my brother's passing on Christmas Day of 1997 left a hole in my heart. I felt totally devastated by it all because I ended up losing all that time that I could have taken to love him, to know him, and to share life and experiences with him. I irrevocably lost the golden opportunity to be a part of his life, and to allow him to be a part of mine, all because I was angry over an episode that had already passed, and which, in any case, could no longer be resolved, even if any need for that even remotely remained. The entire unfortunate sage would mark a remarkable transformation in my life, as today, I live my life on a platform of a refusal to never remain angry with anyone, and about any situation. I no longer hold grudges. I no longer hold ill-will or resentments over incidents that happened in the past. I now find it infinitely easy to forgive, and never hold a grudge, all because I had to learn the hard way that being a grievance holder and collector can cause one to lose so much more than one gains. Anger and bitterness can only take from one, and never add to one. Instructively, I have made it my life mission to preach, each and every single day, to anyone who cares to listen, that nothing destroys the soul as well as cancer destroys the body than holding a grudge. I hasten to add that, just as the words that proceed our mouth simply dissipate into the wind, is how we should allow the so-called awkward and unpleasant occurrences of our life go with the wind. We should simply let go and let live. To go through life collecting and holding on to baggages of incidents as some form of crutch, which is an unnecessary psychic aid at best, and a totally useless appendage at worst, is to live life laboring under a yoke. I labored under that sort of terrible burden for years, and would not wish it for anyone else. My advice is that you simply should not hang on to any such crutches, if only because it will cost you a whole lot more than you really ought to pay. I still pay that premium price for my foolhardiness, on daily basis. That means I am still hurting, and will probably die hurting, all because what I lost, and which now means so much to me, in the form of a relationship with my brother, is something I can never go back to reclaim. Tragically, he was my only brother. My mother had three children. I was the first born, while he was second, with another girl coming after him. Much as I would have really loved to have a relationship with that only brother, it is too late, and it will always remain late. I have only poignant memories to relate with. That is so pathetically empty, and I wish I could have more. Sadly, "more" is not only too late, but totally impossible. Now, I cry every day over my misfortune.

Yet, with the habit of freely forgiving others has come a certain peace of mind. I have discovered that peace of mind is the greatest human good, and that is why, in my relationships, I continually strive towards the point where I can truly honor my peace of mind by realizing that, not only are some battles simply too costly to pursue, but that I must also continue to freely forgive all those I perceive as having offended me. Indeed, peace of mind is also power of mind, for the simple reason that you become truly ready to empower your mind, using the instrumentality of genuine peace. When you finally accept that the very high price at which some battles come can be so prohibitive that you end up being the actual loser, you have finally found true freedom. In fact, I have arrived at the point where I now have the good sense to, on a consistent basis, enquire from myself whether any so-called unpleasant situation is even remotely worth all the attendant fuss and interpersonal acrimony. Because of this merciful insight, I have come to the conclusion that it is nothing more than an exercise in sheer foolishness to pay in excess, far and above the normal price, for any incident in my life. That is why the greatest dividend of the unfortunate fractured relationship that I could not mend before my brother died, and the greatest honor I could possibly offer his memory, is to live a life of peace and harmony, freely forgiving one and all.

It was on the note of the celebration of a new life by my family that I made my entrance into the world barely forty eight hours to Christmas Day of 1959. Yet, the circumstances of my birth was also remarkable for another reason. Barely a year or two after my birth, my native Guyana was thrown into turmoil of the most traumatic coloration. The most significant feature of the socio-political history of Guyana is the issue of race relations. In all fairness, ethnic polarization would ordinarily not have been such a sore point in the history of Guyana. It's just that Guyana has had to endure excruciatingly painful periods when race was used to drive a wedge among the predominant races in Guyana, in particular the Indo-Guyanese and the Afro-Guyanese, who together constitute over 80% of the total population. The rather critical issue of race relations surfaced in the early 1960's when obvious attempts were made to destabilize the PPP administration by western vested interests, in collaboration with local reactionary elements. At the 1963 Independence Conference, the British colonialists had made it clear that they wished to break the political deadlock, and above all, to end the problem of racialism in Guyana which, according to them was the 'curse' of Guyana. They were disenchanted with what they termed 'the development of party politics along racial lines.' This perceived racialism could be traced to the split in the country's main political party in 1955 when the party, which had previously drawn its support from both major races broke into two bitterly opposed political groups, the one predominantly Indian, led by Dr. Jagan, and the other, predominantly African, led by Mr. Burnham.

In essence, the two major racial groups, East Indians and Blacks, took bitterly adversarial positions to each other, and the stage was now set for the tremendous harm that racism and racial conflict would do to the country, despite the well-known fact that Guyanese are by nature a peaceful people who had existed and co-existed peacefully and peaceably with other groups and ethnicities. Before now, there had been little or no evidence of racial segregation in the social life of the country, and East Indians and Africans seemed to mix and associate with one another on very cordial and amiable terms. Without a doubt, hostile and anti-racial sentiments were aroused by the inevitable clash of the hopes and ambitions of rival, unprincipled, and self-seeking politicians. Whatever the antecedents, the elections of August 21st, 1961, became marred with unprecedented violence that was wielded with mind-boggling ferocity along racial lines, and the Indians and Blacks went on an unheard-of killing spree characterized by brutal assault, murder, and arson. Naturally, these unfortunate events only served to divide an already polarized society along racial fissures, laying the foundation for a severe dislocation in the harmonious co-existence of the Blacks and the Indians of Guyana.

It was in the year before the violent elections in Guyana that I was born. That meant I came into the world, as it were, to meet a society bedeviled by severe racial dislocation and tension. My mother, Ena Subryan, was of mixed Indian and Portuguese parentage. My father was Black, while my mother was Indian-Portuguese. She was barely thirteen years of age when she gave birth to me. Put poignantly, it was a classic case of a baby mothering a baby. You will now understand why the title of this book is, "Child of A Child." The young man who had impregnated her, Claude Wesley Josiah, more popularly known as Wesley, my father, was barely seventeen years of age at that time. He was Black. It goes without saying that, for a society that was going through the trauma of terrible racial tensions and fissures, the racial differences between the two teenage lovers was a very sore point for their respective families. In fact, as I later came to realize, the extent of racial disharmony was far in excess of the celebrated racial Black and White dichotomy that the United States was famed for.

After my birth at the small hospital in the township of Mackenzie, the sharp dislocations that would shape my early life came prominently to the fore. My father was Black, while my mother was predominantly Indian, with a trace of Portuguese from her own mother. Wesley's Black family made it quite clear that they wanted nothing to do with Ena's Indo-Portuguese family. Therefore, for all practical purposes, they were laying down the law that they wanted their son to keep his girlfriend and his new-born daughter at arm's length. For such a young couple to be caught up in the vagaries of a racially-divided society must have been terrible indeed. The consequence of this was that Wesley became totally excommunicated from my mother and I, and my father and I only saw each other for the first time many years later.

Interestingly, Wesley always proudly acknowledged the fact that he had a daughter, and in fact sadly fell back on a popular Guyanese folk song to refer to his estranged child. The song went somewhat like this:

```
"I had a girl;
Donna was her name.
Donna my girl;
Oooh, Donna Donna, my girl..."
```

What was most relevant, naturally, in the song was the name 'Donna,' and the young man went around announcing that he had a daughter named Donna. As a result of this, I spent my early years under the mistaken impression that my name was Donna, while in fact it was merely a nickname or alias of sorts.

In the aftermath of the racially violent elections of 1962 in Guyana, in which the erstwhile Indian government was defeated, bringing the Blacks into political reckoning and power, the attendant violence and mutual hatred was so great, with enormous casualties in the Indian and Portuguese communities, that most Indians lost businesses and financial bases that had taken decades to build and nurture. Many of them lost tremendous amounts of physical cash, that era being one in which banking had not gained its present-day popularity. Those that were not out rightly killed would suffer severe physical injuries that sometimes resulted in maiming. My maternal grandfather was in fact beaten black and blue with a bicycle wheel. It was against this background that my maternal grandparents literally fled their accustomed locality in the Guyanese state of Demerara, a predominantly black state, and relocated to Berbice, a predominantly Indian state, where they settled down, and commenced attempts to assume the semblance of a normal life. Having to start life all over again simply meant that a life of poverty stared them fully in the face. In fact, as I recall it, the poverty my maternal grandparents were thrown into was almost unimaginable.

Meanwhile, my mother, Ena, had been rendered totally dysfunctional. This was hardly surprising. A confused thirteen-year-old girl, barely into her teens, she had succumbed to early teen pregnancy, and almost immediately after delivering a child outside wedlock, the father of her child had been unceremoniously yanked out of her life without explanation of any sort. Apart from the fact that she was probably even too young to comprehend the technicalities of the social and racial divisions that had torn her country apart, she only knew that there shouldn't be any conceivable reason why she should be torn away from the man she loved. In the unfortunate event, she became quite a disturbed young girl, and since she was obviously totally disoriented in time and space, she was considered quite unfit to supervise the upbringing of a baby. Therefore, the lot to raise me, her baby, naturally fell on my maternal grandmother, Virginia Subryan, otherwise popularly known as "The Queen."

In the month of April 1959, the year of my birth, my grandmother herself had given birth to her last child, a boy. In effect, that meant Virginia was now saddled with the responsibility of raising two toddlers at the same time. In fact, since they were relocating to Berbice from somewhere else, the impression was, wittingly or unwittingly, created that she had been delivered of twins, a boy and a girl, the two being of approximately the same age and size. So, from this point, I only knew my grandmother as mother, and I would know nothing contrary to this until when I was three years of age when Ena, my biological mother suddenly appeared from seemingly nowhere. That was when I arrived at the knowledge that I had a biological mother, different from my grandmother. In an interesting twist to the tale, Ena would later again have another child, a boy, giving me a biological brother. As it happened, Wesley had been goaded into marriage with another girl by his mother. This marriage broke down, and he married yet another girl. This marriage also did not survive beyond a couple of years. Perhaps in frustration, the hapless young man left Guyana, but not before he had clandestinely impregnated Ena once more. Left all alone again, Ena was in no proper frame of mind to raise her new child. The Amerindians took the child away from her, to go and raise him. In fact, the child had taken severely ill, even as Ena finally succumbed to full-blown alcoholism and total dysfunctionality.

By this time, I had achieved a certain stability and equilibrium in my life with my grandparents. I was in school, but more importantly, I was an outstanding pupil. Even at the age of three years, I had already become a child prodigy of sorts. I was not only performing brilliantly in my studies, but was also already receiving awards for my outstanding performance. That I was a young, bright girl would be putting it mildly. However, I was also growing up in a home in which I was surrounded by young boys. Because of this, my early orientation was to behave and act in a masculine manner, and I became quite competitive. I learned to be tough and resilient, becoming almost a tomboy. In the midst of five young boys, I easily developed an inclination to want to best all my peers in any sphere of activity. My need to become excellent at anything I touched literally became an obsession with me. This is a trait that I would carry into later life, as I would become someone for whom winning became not only second nature, but virtually an obsession.

Over the years, I have often had cause to reflect on my obsession with a competitive urge to win. I once read somewhere that the human urge to win may have its roots in sheer survival, the most basic human drive. In ancient times, if one didn't win against that saber-toothed tiger, or the neighboring tribe, one had really lost, and might not survive the loss. While the pre-historic saber-toothed tiger may be extinct, those primitive feelings haven't gone away, and remain with us. Again, it is said that our desire to win could be related to a chemical in our brain called dopamine, which is linked to pleasure. Besting others not only gives one bragging rights, it also triggers a good feeling in the reward area of one's brain. I think I was simply competitively driven by the primal need to win. Yet, I have often wondered if I didn't see being best as a chance to get better at something by comparing myself to others, or perhaps I saw competition as something that would make me work harder and, in turn, bring out the best in me.

Cousins came visiting at my grandparents' home from all over the country. I easily recall a particular cousin. He was obviously quite wealthy, and anytime he came calling, he was accorded the status of a visiting family celebrity. The entire household would be thrown into a festive mood, as his visits gave the rare occasion for celebration on a massive scale. For some peculiar reason, I was given the impression that this visiting cousin was my father. In innocent ignorance, I swallowed this myth as gospel truth, totally unaware that it was a family joke of sorts. It wasn't until I was about six years of age that I came into the realization that the man was not my father after all. Yet, while the other family members still considered the entire episode an amusing joke, I would develop the unpleasant impression that adults were actually quite wicked, if not altogether callous, to have led me to believe that my cousin was my father, and I would carry this impression of adults as people to be totally distrusted for many years thereafter.

Poverty was a constant feature of my grandparents' home. We were so poor that the very food we ate was, all by itself, a luxury on its own. My grandfather worked as a barber, and his returns on his daily efforts were so meager as to be barely able to support the family. Their only significant respite came from my eldest uncle, who worked as an electrician at a big bauxite plant. It was this uncle who virtually supplied all the feeding needs of the entire family. Despite all this, I retain very warm memories of my maternal grandfather. William Subryan was an extraordinarily disciplined individual who ran his household in accordance with a particularly strict code of rules. His protocol was so rigid that it almost bordered on the regimental. He insisted that things had to be done in a certain way. Even at that, certain things had to be done in accordance with a particular regimen from which one couldn't veer. Looked at from a superficial viewpoint, it would appear as if the old man was too authoritarian, but in actual fact it allowed for the running of his household in an orderly fashion which somewhat took the bite out the grinding poverty to which it was subjected. Put differently, the man had painstakingly insinuated a clear structure into the day-to-day life of the members of his household. For instance, I had specific times for doing school work, house chores and play time. It was a rigid routine that I eventually came to become intimately familiar with, and which governed every fiber of my being as I grew into a young girl with my grandparents. When one added this to the fact that I was performing spectacularly well at school, it was clear that a magnificent foundation was being laid for a life of industry and purpose.

Grandfather William was a particularly fastidious person. It hardly comes as surprise that I have evolved into the kind of person that I am today, living a life structured along the lines of daily living with single-minded purpose, discipline, uncommon industry and rare success-orientation. I imbibed all these sterling qualities from my early exposure to the structured manner of living that William Subryan instilled in all those who lived under his roof. In many respects, it was an absolutely fascinating study in positive and proactive communal living. Members of the household were trained to hold certain values very dear. For instance, we all had breakfast together unfailingly at

6am every morning, and gathered together for at 6pm for dinner. Lunch was not a part of this unwavering routine only because most people were either out at school, or at work. Quite apart from this dinning culture, Grandfather William also instituted a unique program of family interaction in which we all gathered together at least four nights of every week to share personal experiences. This forum would usually require one person to tell some unique personal story to the others, and then there would be a hearty discussion around it which might involve words of encouragement or advice. Naturally, these interactions also served as platforms for everyone to gain some wisdom or the other from the experiences of others.

Another rather unique quality of my grandfather was the pedestal of dual respect and affection on which he placed his wife, Virginia, my grandmother. Despite his strict and foreboding orientation, he was devoted to his wife, almost to the point of veneration. He attended to her every need with scrupulous attention, and would always make sure that she remained in a happy state of mind at all times. I recall that I took particular note of the deep respect that the man displayed towards his wife, and that is probably why today, I have grown into a person who makes it a point to respect and cherish the people in my life. This idyllic, though poverty-ridden state of affairs would continue until I was around seven years of age, when my dysfunctional biological mother, Ena, suddenly materialized in Berbice. Apparently, my father, Wesley, who had been away from Guyana for quite some time, had come back into the country with his current wife, a Trinidadian. Ena, apparently seeking whatever means at her disposal to maintain close ties with Wesley, came up with the seemingly ingenious scheme of integrating me into my biological father's life. And so, one fine Saturday morning, she suddenly appeared and requested her mother to release me to her for a visit to my father in Linden. Virginia's hands were tied in the face of this perfectly defensible request. She certainly could proffer no valid argument to prevent me from meeting my biological father. Wesley had done fairly well for himself in life. He was considered, by all local standards, a reasonably wealthy man. He lived in a big, spacious home with his wife and mother, who still exerted tremendous influence on him. In addition to these three people, four children lived in the house. They were the children of Wesley's sister who had died a few years earlier. Therefore, to all intents and purposes, the responsibility for raising the four girls had now fallen on the young man, and from all indications, Salome, my paternal grandmother, had decided to strategically position the girls to be in line to inherit their uncle's estate. Although she carefully concealed her scheming from her son, successfully masking, at least in the initial stages, her total resentment of what she perceived to be my unwelcome intrusion into their lives, it was clear that the elderly woman did not happily receive me into her son's home. The baby she had earlier rejected had by now grown into a bright, respectful and promising young girl, and Grandmother Salome saw me as nothing short of a potential threat to her scheme to see that the four girls occupied a place of unrivaled prominence in the affections of her son. As it were, I would spend an unforgettable two-week vacation at my father's big house, a far cry from the poverty in which I was living in Berbice. To say that I was totally entranced with this new lease of life would be an understatement. I was seeing another side to life that I never knew existed, and I simply lapped up all the perks of luxury. When it was time for me to leave, as I was due to go back and take my Common Entrance Examinations to high school, it was with mixed feelings of regret and longing that were somewhat assuaged by the gifts of new clothes and a jar of valuable nickels I was given as a parting gift by a grandmother who was only too glad to see me leave anyway. The jar of nickels came in very useful for my private purchases of sweets and other menial fancies that were common with young girls of my age.

The next year, my father repeated his visit to Guyana, and my mother once more came to Bernice to retrieve me for yet another visit to my father's house. If on the first visit, I was fascinated by the ambiance in my father's house, this time around I was completely entranced, and at the starry-eyed age of eight years, I probably came to the momentous decision that I was not going back to the life of grinding poverty at Berbice. When my stay at my father's house was seemingly become interminable, grandmother Virginia came from

Berbice to reclaim me. She met the shock of her life. I would not budge from my father's house. I did not mince my words in informing my maternal grandmother that I was finally here to stay. I recall my grandmother standing on the veranda of the big house, looking very forlorn and sad, and pleading with me to come back to Berbice with her. I adamantly refused. The lure of luxury proved too tempting to abandon. Grandmother Virginia dissolved into tears. I stared at the older woman in disbelief. I couldn't understand why the woman was not happy that I was now in my own father's very comfortable home, with all the material comfort that went with it. Virginia wept uncontrollably, and in between body-wracking sobs, told me that I would later regret my decision. But, I simply could not understand why I would be willing to give up a mansion that had six rooms, three bathrooms and numerous other facilities for the, at least in my perception, hovel we were all inhabiting in Berbice. The poor lady turned back, leaving me to what she instinctively knew was a foreboding fate. A new and eventful phase had started in my life. Grandmother Virginia would be proved uncannily right.

2

The Child Slave

"Children require guidance and sympathy far more than
instruction." - Anne Sulivan

Virginia Subryan left me in peace at my father's house in Linden, and returned
to join her family in Berbice. She had arrived Linden full of expectations
that we would return to Berbice together. She had not expected the sudden
transformation in me, from her little, contented country girl, to one who
was now totally enamored and entrapped with the trappings of wealth and
affluence. As the popular saying goes, poverty is an orphan. In my own
case, my previous poverty was an innocent orphan, and now, with the taste
of the finer things life had on palatable offer, the scales of innocence had
seemingly fallen from my eyes, and I had now become a fairy tale princess
living the dream of a life I never even knew existed in the first place. My
story might have borne a striking resemblance to that of Cinderella, the
popular character in fairy tale fiction, were it not for certain differences, the
most significant of which was that, instead of the stepmother in Cinderella's
story, I had my own paternal grandmother to reckon with.

The long and short of the story was that my maternal grandmother, Virginia

Subryan, reluctantly left me behind in Linden, and she left a very sad woman indeed. That turn in events would mark the remarkable beginning to an ironic twist to a young life that had hitherto been characterized by real poverty, yet a relatively blissful childhood. In truth, at that stage of my life, I was understandably in total ignorance of the details of my father's life. What I did not know, in the blissful ignorance of a young girl entranced by her own fairy tale, was that my father was not permanently resident in Guyana. It is, of course, debatable whether knowledge of this fact might have swayed me from what was to later turn out the ill-advised decision to abandon my maternal grandparents in favor of my father's home. Wesley, my father, had actually become a dual resident of Canada and the United States of America at this time. He divided his time abroad between those two counties, but would often return home, usually four times in a year to recharge his family batteries, so to speak, and perhaps to invest his expatriate earnings in his now burgeoning business interests in Guyana. He was quite wealthy, even by Afro-Guyanese standards. He was a dentist. He was also a goldsmith. To cap an exciting business career, he owned one of the most successful social clubs in Guyana. The club served the dual purpose of a bar restaurant, and a rendezvous point for local residents to unwind and interact.

Within a couple of weeks of my taking up permanent residency at my father's house, his current Guyanese vacation came to an end, and he returned to the United States. While I did not actually envisage his departure, there being no need for him to intimate me, a young child, of his travel plans, on my own part, there really was no reason for me to have been unduly bothered since, certainly up till the time of his departure, nothing could be said to be amiss in the ambience of my new environment. At that time, I had, shortly before departing Bernice, just taken the Common Entrance Examination that would usher me into high school education. Not unexpectedly, I had done exemplarily well in the examinations, so much so that I won a scholarship to a junior high school. In those salutary circumstances, all that was expected from me was to be fully kitted with my recommended textbooks and school uniforms. With my father's departure, back to his American base, the lot, not unnaturally, to attend to my needs fell on a grandmother who might be safely assumed to have been adequately funded by her departing son to ensure the comfortable upkeep of his daughter. Suffice it to say that it was at this point that my world turned, not only upside down, but entered a free fall of one disaster after the other at the hands of my paternal grandmother.

It is natural for us to to think of grandmothers as kindly, caring, and supportive. Certainly, while my father was with us at Linden, his mother was the epitome of love and affection, and nothing could have even remotely prepared me for the sudden transformation of my grandmother into the very personification of evil as soon as my father's back was turned. Yet, can we really say we are unfamiliar with evil grandmothers in the annals of human history? Any student of biblical history will be familiar with the story of Athaliah, Queen of Judah. Anytime I think of Grandmother Salome, and just how evil a grandmother can elect to be, I remember this story. In what can only be described as a 'night of the long knives,' an idiomatic representation of ruthless and treacherous action against others, screams from the unwilling witnesses of unspeakable horror rang out from the darkened rooms and gloomy corridors of the vast, ancient palace. People ran helter skelter in utter confusion. The only people who appeared safe, secure and assured were the silent merchants of death, who went about their gruesome assignment with uncommon grimness of purpose. Soon enough, strident shrieks of "Assasin! Assasin!" rent the air.

An hour later, an uneasy quiet descended on the palace. The deed was done. The ignominious mission was accomplished to the total satisfaction of its sponsor. Athaliah, Queen Mother of Judah, had done both the unthinkable, and the unspeakable. She had just murdered her four grandsons. Let us take the story from the beginning. Athaliah was royalty personified. She was the daughter of a king. She was the wife of a king. She was the mother of a king. In fact, in the long and turbulent history of Judah, the latter-day successor to the United Monarchy of Israel under the biblical Kings Saul, Solomon and David, she was the only sovereign queen of that kingdom. In those days, King Ahab ruled over Judah. His wife was Queen Jezebel. As a royal couple, they not only personified evil, but celebrated it to the crudest point of bestiality. Athaliah, their daughter, raised her parents' benchmark of evil to a new and exotic level, gloriously and totally insinuating idolatry into the very fabric of Jewish society. Ahaziah was her son, and he became King after his father, King Jeroham, but ruled for only a year.

Athaliah, the Queen Mother, in her quest to bypass the normal protocol of ascension, and usurp the throne for herself, murdered her own grandsons, the children of her son. After this gruesome act, Athaliah reigned for six years. While her husband reigned, she was the power *behind* the throne. Now, she was the power *on* the throne. Yet, poetic justice would soon be served. Unknown to Athalia, as she set out to massacre all her grandsons, the youngest of the princes was saved from the orgy of annihilation by the sheer contrivance of an ingenious palace conspiracy. The young prince, Joash, was hidden away by his aunt. When he attained the age of seven years of age, a very subterranean, yet equally successful, conspiratorial effort was executed to install the boy on the throne as the lawful king of Judah. As the coronation of Joash was taking place in the temple in Jerusalem, Athaliah, the boy's grandmother, got wind of the clandestine affair, and stormed the venue, frantically screaming, "Treason! Treason!" But it was too late. The palace coup had been successfully plotted and executed, and a crown was already on the head of the new king. Grandmother Athaliah was cut down by the swords of the guards just outside the temple door. Her lifeless body was left unattended to in an ignominious end to an equally ignominious reign. In consistence with prophecy, Athaliah's death would bear a singularly striking, if not totally uncanny resemblance to that of her mother, Jezebel, whose corpse was abandoned outside the gates of the city of Jerusalem for wild dogs to ravage. Athaliah, her daughter was left to be trampled upon by horses at the temple gates.

The unbridled lust for power and selfish self-interest has, for centuries, been mankind's greatest undoing, coming second after only the avaricious pursuit of illicit wealth. As soon as our entire existence seeks validation only from a reference point of evil power over others, our concept and perception of influence in the lives of others will be fundamentally flawed, leading to a quest for the gratification of our own self-interest at any cost, no matter how prohibitive that price may be. In its classic definition, power is the capacity or ability to have direct influence on others, or, in the corollary, the ability or capacity to alter the course of events in the lives of others. Contrary to popular misconception, true and legitimate power is the inalienable right of every one of us. Quite possibly, the very real power dilemma might be explicable on the basis of a total misapprehension of what true power and its application connotes in the affairs of others. Rather than oppressing others, we must continually seek ways to add quantifiable value to their lives by becoming the epitome of selflessness. In sacrosanct truth, the true power that our Creator endowed us with has nothing to do with the oppression of others.

My own grandmother became my oppressor. As soon as my father left Guyana at the end of that vacation, Grandmother Salome unleashed a reign of terror on me, her own grandchild. Grandmother Salome bluntly refused to send me to school. Her rather spurious and illegitimate claim was that she did not have the money for my schooling. To add inglorious color to a tale that was already taking on a rather gruesome hue, from that point onwards, my grandmother systematically embarked upon a scheme to turn me into her house maid. It was also at that point that my grandmother's ignominious agenda became obvious. That agenda was simply to totally eliminate all possibility of me becoming an inheritor of my father's estate and legacy. Clearly, Grandmother Salome perceived me as coming from a background that was so intimidating to her own world that I presented nothing but a real threat to her carefully laid out plans for her late daughter's children.

As it were, I was coming from a background in which I had been subjected to a structured and disciplined upbringing. My maternal grandparents at

Berbice had taught to me be respectful and industrious. When you added these traits to my naturally bright and sharp juvenile intellect, you were presented with the enduring picture of the quintessential golden girl. In sharp contrast to these perceivably enviable characteristics in me were the three girls that my father's sister had left behind upon her sad demise. Obviously, to Grandmother Salome, in contrast to my own intriguing mixture of Black, Indian and Portuguese features, my cousins were a total antithesis of all she would have wished for her late daughter's children. In sharp contrast to me, the girls were unruly, rude, lazy and spoilt rotten by their grandmother. The sharp distinction between the girls and I was not lost on Salome. It was also quite clear to her that in a fair competition for favor in the eyes of her son, I would win hands down. Yet, she was determined that I would have no share in the inheritance of her son's estate.

It was a rather chaotic household, and a far cry from what I had been accustomed to. My deceased aunt had actually left four children behind, and they included a boy and three girls. The boy was the eldest child and was away from home, since he was probably old enough to fend for himself. The three girls were an incorrigible trio, and the worst of their traits appeared to find concentration in gross proportion in the eldest girl, Brenda, who would later turn out a complete vagrant. Brenda would also later take to stealing. She would steal money from her uncle's business, and even when she was caught literally with her hand in the till, her grandmother would collude with the police to let her off the hook. She later became so belligerent that she not only became associated with local gangs, but also got into very violent street fights. In all these, my grandmother appeared quite content to turn a blind eye. Worse, the girls would not leave me to exist peacefully in my own corner. I possessed only a very few clothes, which I tried to preserve as neatly as possible. The other girls would invade my box, and steal my clothes, and either never returned them, or at best, subjected them to the worst possible treatment.

It wasn't so long before my father came home on another vacation. By this time, I had virtually turned into the home's resident cook. This was quite apart from having to do a multiplicity of other household chores like sweeping, dusting and washing. I was also required to keep an eye on returns from the club business downstairs, because my grandmother had to grudgingly admit that I was the only one who could be trusted with the business money. An eloquent example of what I had to endure presented itself one day with regards to my father's food. Usually, after cooking, I would place my father's food on the dining table and cover it with a heavy towel to keep it warm. Half of the time, my father would have eaten out anyway, and when he returned, he would ask the girls to eat his food. However, at other times, especially if he had not eaten out, he would be looking forward to his own food at home. One day, the very belligerent eldest of her cousins, Brenda, probably not anticipating that her uncle would express interest in his food, stealthily ate a good portion of it, and covered the rest. As fate would have it, however, her uncle came back home hungry, only to discover that his food was half eaten already. Angry at the discovery, he couldn't get anyone to own up to the misdemeanor. Finally, he declared that everyone would get a beating, since the culprit was not willing to own up. At this decision, I decided to take the blame, to save the others from the mass punishment. But my father was not fooled. He knew only too well that his daughter was not the culprit, and because of this he changed his initial decision to punish everyone.

Shortly after this incident, my father's vacation came to an end, and he went back to Canada. At his departure, my infamous career as a child slave commenced in earnest. It might appear rather dramatic to describe myself as a child slave in my own father's house, but in truth, that was what I was. After all, slavery is a situation in which someone appears owned by and made to work for another person without having any say over what happens to them. A slave is held against their own will and is not allowed to leave or to refuse to work. Child slavery has serious short- and long-term consequences. Almost invariably, it is also attended by emotional and physical abuse. I was just a child, and it was extremely difficult for me to really comprehend why I had to be in such a terrible situation in my own father's house. Naturally, it was also very hard for me to psychologically deal with what I was experiencing, both physically and mentally.

I was required to clean all the rooms in the big house, from upstairs to downstairs. I cooked all the meals eaten in the house. I did all the laundry. Let me rephrase that, as it somehow glamorizes that rather arduous chore. I washed all the dirty clothes, and there were literally loads of them, as my cousins seemingly appeared to take a perverse pleasure in accumulating dirty laundry, from one day to the next, knowing only too well that their slaving cousin was always there to clean up after them. I swept all around the house perimeter to keep the grounds clean. To add to an already huge domestic burden, if the supplies of liquor to the club came in short supply, I was required to go out to make emergency purchases, and I would have to convey a couple of crates of liquor back home on my head. While the other girls had many school uniforms, I had only one set of uniforms. I was rather fastidious about my clothes, and I would wash my uniform, dry it, and then fold the shirt very neatly under my pillow so as to make it look ironed after a few hours. Early in the morning, however, I was burdened with so much work that I barely had time to quickly prepare for school. What was more tragic was that my lazy cousins would often go under my pillow and take my neat uniform, and wear them to school, leaving me with no choice than to rapidly wash one of their own dirty uniforms, and wear it in that wet state to school.

Quite often, Grandmother Salome's unfair treatment of me was taken to malevolent lengths. One day, at the height of preparations for a house party, she sent my eldest cousin, Brenda, to the market to purchase new clothes that everyone would wear at the party, and although she issued specific instructions as to details of the purchase very much to my hearing, she did not include me in her calculations. It just so happened that this particular incident coincided with one of my father's visits to Guyana. Shortly before the party started, my father noticed that, while the other girls wore obviously new dresses, I was wearing one of the old dresses he had brought for me on a previous visit from overseas. Not satisfied with my reserved response to his enquiry, he questioned his wife, who gave the rather feeble excuse that at the time the purchases were to be made from the market, I was absent from home, and that was why I was not included in the estimates. Although, not that it made any significant difference to my untenable circumstances, since he was out of the country most of the time, perhaps at this stage, my father started to notice that his daughter was being treated, not as his own daughter ought to be treated, but like a pariah.

In many respects, I had a rather complicated father-daughter relationship with my father. Perhaps matters might have turned out differently had he spent more time in Guyana at that critical stage of my life. Yet, I do know that part of the reason why I was only too keen to forgo life in Berbice with my maternal grandparents, apart from a life of newly discovered comfort and luxury, was the subconscious security I found in living in my father's house. We hear a lot about the importance of male role models in a boy's life. It is indeed important. But what's often missing from the narrative is the importance of a father in a daughter's life as well. As part of the lessons I would like to bequeath in this book, I will dwell a bit on my own perception of the psychology of father-daughter relationships.

Children really do learn from what they witness. Not having the perspective of older people, they consider whatever their family is like as their "normal." From infancy, girls draw conclusions about what men are like from the men in their life. If there is a father, or a male in her life who assumes a father's role, that man becomes her guidepost for what to expect of men, and what to expect of men's attitude toward women. His relationship to her mother, or his significant other, is her template for what her relationship with a man will be as an adult. For me, this particular factor draws some significance from how my paternal grandfather related with his wife. A rather unique quality of Grandfather William reflected in the respect and affection with which he treated his wife, Virginia, my grandmother, and the obvious high esteem in which he held her. Despite his foreboding disposition as a strict disciplinarian, he was, almost to the point of veneration, devoted to his wife. He attended to her every need with uncommon devotion, ensuring that she was as happy as anyone could possibly be. My grandfather's consideration and respect for his wife made a remarkable impression on my young mind, and that is probably why I have grown into a person who makes it a scrupulous point of obligation to respect and cherish everyone in my life.

Such early learnings are extremely powerful. Regardless of what happens as a teen and adult, a girl who identifies her gender as female has already created a set of assumptions of what it means for her to be a woman by the time she is four or five years old. At each stage of her development, she is watching and learning from both the women and men around her to figure out how to be successful as a woman, and how to be in a relationship with a man. When that learning is positive and helpful for negotiating the world, a daughter will grow up to be at ease in her own skin and in her own sexuality. When it is conflicted or creates expectations that are demeaning or less than useful for cooperating with others, her relationship with herself, with other women, and with men will become troubled. What all this means for a father, or a father figure, is that he counts a lot in the life of his daughter. Regardless of whether he wants the responsibility, a father's relationship to the world and to women sets down a template that will be played out for another generation. Men who take their job as the father of a girl seriously are men who know the importance of certain important things in the life of a young girl. For instance, a young girl needs her father to love her mother. This is the most important thing a man can do. If you can't love her mother, find something to respect and admire in her anyway. With a high divorce rate and equally high never-married-single-parent rate, we must acknowledge that not all parents are bound by love. Yet, however a father feels emotionally about a girl's mother, it is in his and the child's best interests for him to treat the mother with respect and consideration, no matter the domestic circumstances. Even if the mother doesn't return the favor, he can live an honorable life that shows his daughter that a man takes the high road when it comes to his respect for women and his responsibilities to his children.

A father should allow his daughter to attach to him. Girls with a solid sense of self are often their father's very good friend, at least for a while when growing up. A father should spend regular quality time with his daughter. Girls are just as keen on engaging in boisterous outdoor activities with their fathers as boys are. A father should also celebrate his daughter's mind. A father should read to his little girl. He should be interested in what she is learning at school. He should pay attention to her interests, and be honestly curious to learn what she knows about them. He should share interesting things with her about his work and his hobbies. Research shows that the most successful women have generally had fathers who were interested in their intellect and their interests. In the final analysis, a little girl needs her father in her life. I did not have that privilege. Perhaps if I had, my grandmother would not have had the dubious privilege of converting me to her slave child.

3

Little Girl Lost

"No matter how old she may be, sometimes a girl just needs her mom." - Cardinal Mermillod

My school principal was a rather nice and congenial lady named Ms. Lane. She couldn't help but take note of the unusual brightness of the quiet, young girl who came to school with so much sadness in her eyes. Ms. Lane did all in her power to encourage me. One of the steps she took was to enroll me for what, in Guyana, was called the Preliminary Examinations, something akin to an examination taken in the Junior High School in the United States. When she discovered that I could not produce the entry fee for the examinations, which hardly came as a surprise as Grandmother Salome bluntly declared that she couldn't afford it, Ms. Lane went the extra mile to pay for my entry for the examination. As fate would have it, Ms. Lane and Grandmother Salome belonged to the same political party. At the next meeting of party members, Ms. Lane informed Salome that she had paid my examination fees, as the closing date was imminent, and demanded a refund of the fees. When my grandmother arrived home, livid with anger at what she termed my embarrassment of her before her political friends, she descended on me, and visited a most horrendous beating on me. She concluded my ordeal by excommunicating me from the house, asking me to sleep outside the house.

Instructively, my first expulsion from the house had been milder than this. In that incident, which was as a result of a perceived minor misdemeanor, most probably an instance of shifting the blame of theft of money from the restaurant from Brenda to me, Grandmother Salome had merely asked me to sleep on the building's verandah, which still proved a relatively habitable point of exile. This recent expulsion was, however, more drastic, as my grandmother actually ordered me to leave the building itself, and I found myself walking the streets. Pathetically distraught and hungry, without a clue as to my next destination, I ran into a young man who was a regular patron of my father's restaurant and bar in the lower floor of my father's house. The man, named Lennox Holder, felt some sympathy for me, and took me to stay with him in his house. Feeling pathetically grateful for the respite, I followed him home. Lennox was very kind to me, and contrary to what might have been ordinarily expected in such circumstances, he made to attempt whatsoever to sexually exploit me.

All went well for a couple of days, until a friend of his came calling. Looking at me, he casually remarked that I was a strikingly pretty girl. I smiled at the young man, in clear appreciation of the compliment. Shortly after Lennox's friend left, he descended on me, and gave me a severe beating, in obvious anger at my smiling response to his friend's compliment. It was a particularly brutal beating, and it left me with a totally traumatized face and bleeding nostrils. Worse, he refused to give me anything to eat, and left me for work without any provision for my feeding. In abject hunger, I strolled out of the house in search of sustenance, and in the process was spotted by a couple of cousins who scurried off to report my traumatized state to my grandmother. They threatened to write my father to report his daughter's pathetic condition to him if she did not admit me back into the house and take proper care of me. Alarmed at this prospect, Grandmother Salome asked them to go and fetch me, and I was resettled once more in my father's house.

32

My life resumed pretty much the usual pattern of gross domestic abuse, with me doing all the work at the house, while running errands to keep the restaurant and bar well stocked, and barely managing to squeeze in my schooling in between. A couple of months later, my father came on another vacation from his overseas base. He came with his new wife, a Trinidadian. However, in contrast to his previous visits which would usually last only three weeks at the lengthiest, he was compelled to stay three months on this one. The immediate and compelling reason for this protracted visit was that his new wife was involved in a domestic accident that resulted in severe orthopedic trauma. She fell down the staircase and broke a leg.

This domestic accident was to inaugurate an entirely new set of agonizing events in my young life. Guyana is very much like most most other countries in the Caribbean, where fundamentally African antecedents all but guaranteed a belief in most things surreal, esoteric, and possibly, with fetish undertones. Like any other society that held superstition at a revered and respected premium, it was not unusual for local Guyanese residents to consult an *obeah* practitioner on a regular basis. Obeah is a term used in the West Indies to refer to sorcery and religious practices developed among West African slaves, specifically of Igbo and Ashanti origins in West Africa. Obeah is widely practiced in Guyana, and is associated with both benign and malignant magic, charms, luck, and with mysticism in general. An obeah practitioner is, more often than not, referred to as a witch. Such a witch would usually ingeniously combine the skills of a fetish physician with that of a seer, and that of a prophet, all rolled in one. Almost invariably, any misadventure, mishap or accident, usually attracted a visit to this local witch, usually for the combined purpose of identifying the culprit responsible for the unfortunate event, and perhaps also to prescribe some ameliorating recipe or treatment. As it happened, Grandmother Salome had such a practitioner on her retainer. She was a locally eminent woman named Ms. Blue.

For the benefit of the uninitiated, I will dwell a little bit on Obeah, so that the reader can contextually grasp its essence with regard to my story. Obeah is also a series of African diasporic spell-casting and healing traditions found in the former British colonies of the Caribbean. These traditions derive most of their core beliefs from traditional West African practices that have undergone cultural transformation over the centuries. There is much regional variation in the practice of Obeah, which is followed by practitioners called *Obeahmen* and *Obeahwomen,* who faithfully serve a range of clients in assisting them with their problems. A central role is played by healing practices, often incorporating herbal and animal ingredients. It often also involves measures designed to achieve justice for the client. These practices often make reference to supernatural forces, which is why Obeah is sometimes characterized as a religious practice. Obeah actually developed among African communities in the diaspora, in the various British Caribbean colonies following the Atlantic slave trade of the 16th to 19th centuries. It evolved through the adaptation of the traditional religious practices that enslaved West Africans, especially from the Ashanti tribe of the former Gold Coast, now known as Ghana, brought to these colonies. As Ebenezer Morgan White, a renowned Obeah expert once wrote,

```
"Obeah is power. It is a belief. An African tradition. A human
tradition. Obeah is Egyptian. Obeah is Ashanti. Obeah is Hebrew.
Obeah is Jamaican. Many statements can describe Obeah but all
will only touch upon small facets. They are the reflective faces
of a diamond. We see only what is shown back if we gaze into one
face."
```

In those British Caribbean colonies, the enslaved Africans also absorbed European influences, especially from Christianity, the religion of the British colonialists. These British elites, not unexpectedly, disapproved of African traditional religions and introduced various laws to curtail and prohibit them. This suppression meant that Obeah emerged as a system of practical rituals and procedures, rather than as a broader religious system involving deity worship and communal rites. In this respect, Obeah differs from more worship-focused African religions in the Caribbean, such as *Haitian Voodoo,* or even *Jamaican Myal.* However, since the 1980s, Obeah's practitioners have campaigned to remove legal restrictions against their practices in various Caribbean countries, and variants of Obeah are still practiced throughout the Caribbean Community of nations.

In Obeah tradition, it is typically believed that practitioners are born with special powers. They are often referred to as having been *"born with the gift."* It is believed that possession of these powers may be revealed to the individual through dreams or visions in late childhood or early adolescence. Also, it is sometimes believed that an Obeah practitioner will bear a physical disability, such as a blind eye, a club foot, or a deformed hand, and that their powers are a compensation for this. Traditionally, it is often believed that Obeah powers pass hereditarily from a parent to their eldest child. Alternatively, it is believed someone may become a practitioner following a traumatic event in their life. Once they have decided to pursue the practice, a person typically becomes the apprentice of an established Obeahman or woman, and this apprenticeship can last up to five or six years. An Obeah practitioner's success with attracting clients is usually based on a reputation cultivated over years.

Ultimately, Obeah sat at the intersection of politics and spirituality, and has been described as the "magical art of resistance," because it gave its practitioners and its clients a sense of empowerment in the face of oppression, especially slavery and colonialism. Despite the constraints and violence of colonial rule, many obeah practitioners assumed positions of power within their communities and were respected and revered, by both their communities and European colonialists who feared the power of obeah. In summary, so that the reader can fully understand the context in which it features in my unfolding story, Obeah is often understood to follow two interrelated paths in its practice. The first path falls within the realm of the *'supernatural,'* and it involves the art of casting spells, the warding off of evil, the conjuring of luck and wealth, and the protection of oneself and others. The colonialists recognized this path as threatening to their control of enslaved people, given that this supernatural power was often wielded in the name of retaliation for violence against enslaved Africans. This shift of power and fear is integral to understanding obeah as a means of resistance.

The second path of obeah concerns medical authority and involves the knowledge and use of certain plants and animal products to heal illnesses, albeit in a manner not given credence by the British colonialists. This set of knowledge practices was likely influenced by Indigenous Caribbeans, who had profound knowledge of the medicinal benefits of Caribbean plants. This aspect of obeah was generally seen as less threatening than its supernatural force. Quite frankly, Obeah, the black magic of the Caribbean, was, and is still, considered effective, both in matters of life and death, and in the day-to-day affairs of the people. A person might turn to Obeah if he malevolently wishes to destroy his competitor's business, or if he wants to clinch a promotion at work, or if he needs a spell that will make him irresistible to the opposite sex.

It was to Obeah that Grandmother Salome turned in her search of the ubiquitous culprit that would take the blame for her daughter-in-law's misfortune. Shortly after the accident that resulted in the fracture of the latter's leg, Grandmother Salome ceremoniously took her daughter-in-law for a consultation with Ms. Blue, her obeahwoman. After the usual mysterious juggling of multiple fetish objects, the witch looked very solemnly at my grandmother.

"What I am about to tell you is not good news for your home at all."

"Tell me," Salome replied ominously.

"That little girl in your house....what's her name?......Monica?.......She is a little, wicked witch. She has ganged up with her mother, who is also a witch, to cause your daughter-in-law this grievous harm. If you do not take steps to remove her from your house, there is every possibility that her attack may lead to someone's death."

That was all Grandmother Salome needed to put a nail in my coffin of woes. They hurried home to reveal their findings to my father. As might be totally expected, Grandmother Salome exaggerated her report in the most dramatic manner conceivable, and if the poor, hapless man had any reservations whatsoever about a report that totally weighed against his own daughter, his hands were irrevocably tied by his wife's declaration that her husband had to choose between me and herself. The die was cast. One person had to leave the house. My father broke the shattering news to me. I had to leave. I had to go to live with my mother. The tone of finality in his voice brooked no protestations to the contrary. I had irrevocably lost in my battle of wits with my paternal grandmother.

This would not be the first time Grandmother Salome would be sending me on exile to live with my mother. A year before this, shortly after I had come to live at my father's house, and barely a couple of months following his return overseas after his vacation in Guyana, Grandmother Salome had latched onto a very flimsy excuse to throw me out of the house. Brenda, the eldest of my cousins, as I previously mentioned, was an incorrigible thief, apart from being a veritable expert at a host of other juvenile vices. She had grown into the unsavory habit of stealing money from the sales made at the restaurant and club downstairs. The truth was that Grandmother Salome was well aware of her granddaughter's escapades, but curiously chose to turn a blind eye to them. In any case, she had opted to spoil the girls rotten. On this particular occasion, Brenda had stolen a whopping twenty thousand dollars, and that was quite a substantial sum, even for a restaurant that was making a lot of money on daily basis. When the theft became public knowledge, Salome, as usual, chose to divert suspicion from Brenda by pointing accusing fingers at me. I denied the theft, but it was all to no avail, as my grandmother had decided to make me the 'fall guy,' as they say. It was at that point that her ultimate agenda became clear. She used the perceived gravity of the offense to send me on exile, to go and live with my mother.

At this time, Ena, my mother, was in the most pathetic state of dysfunction imaginable. She was a child trying to be a mother to children like herself. Having had me at the very tender age of thirteen, she was little more than a child herself. What threw her over the edge was her totally inexplicable separation from the man she loved, and had become pregnant for. She never quite came to terms with her forced estrangement from her childhood sweetheart, and with nowhere else to turn to for succor, she found ready solace in chronic alcoholism. Hers was a particularly pathetic existence in those days. My forced exile to go and live with my mother was to open my eyes to the terrible state of affairs in which my biological mother was. To even attempt a comparison between Ena's living conditions and the luxurious ambience at Wesley's home would be to indulge in the totally ridiculous, as they were two worlds at diametric opposites sides of the human spectrum.

Ena lived in a decrepit and run down tenement building that was composed of hundreds of rooms. She lived in one of these rooms, which was little more than a hovel. The room, which served as the entire apartment, was about the size of a small kitchen. The room provided barely enough space for human movement, and the toilet facilities were outside, shared by the other occupants of the building. At night, you would spread old clothing on the floor to serve as a makeshift bed, and in the morning you would fold those old clothes back into the box, to turn the room into a living room. There was a one-burner stove in the corner for the minimal amount of cooking you could do. The room had a door, and one window. There was a little stand at the window where you would wash the dishes. The entire building itself was constructed with wood, and such a shoddy job was done of its construction that there were large, yawning gaps in both the floor boards and the walls. Curtains had to be hung up to cover the gaps in the walls to ensure some semblance of privacy from prying eyes. What, however, could not be kept out were the huge rodents that scampered randomly throughout the building at all times. The building was infested with a population of rats that could be compared with what you saw in the underground sewers of a large city. It was common to feel the rats run over one's body while sleeping on the floor at night. This was the grossly deplorable condition in which I found my mother when I was forced to go and live with her.

Ena's lifestyle, not surprisingly, mirrored her decrepit living conditions with uncanny precision. You had this young girl who had been torn away from the relationship that resulted in a love child, and by circumstances that she could not even begin to understand. She was an emotional wreck, and spent all her waking hours in an alcoholic haze. Her days followed the same dysfunctional pattern. She would spend the early part of the day crawling from one rum shop to the other, drinking. At such places, being a remarkably attractive young girl, she would attract the attention of young, vagrant males, who invariably paid for her drinking binges. Not unnaturally, another distressing aspect of this lifestyle that I witnessed was the frequent visits of these men to our small room, where in that constrained space, Ena was compelled to accord sexual favors to her patrons. Naturally, nothing could be worse for a young girl to experience than this. Usually, in the later part of the day, Ena would expend her little sums of money on visits to the movie theatre. She was particularly fond of movies, and late at night, she would crawl back home in the worst drunken state imaginable, more often than not in the garrulous company of one of her regular patrons, to cap the night with illicit sex, in the presence of her innocent daughter.

I recall all these gory details with uncommon compassion and understanding for my mother. I believe that, to this day, compassion remains the only basis on which I can continue to view the rather tragic life of my mother. Thankfully, compassion has also emerged a key component of my view of humanity as a whole, as it allows me to continue to appreciate the tenuous cord of love that is supposed to bind us all together. Certainly, I am of the view that compassion allows our heart to beat in synchrony with other hearts, such that, we not only gain access into those hearts, but their despairing and agonizing contents are also revealed to us. Most people understandably equate compassion with kindness. However, the scope of the meaning and application of compassion goes far beyond mere kindness, which is only a composite of compassion. Compassion involves the willingness to do four things. One; Put yourself in someone else's shoes. Two; Take the focus off yourself. Three; Imagine what it's like to be in someone else's predicament. Four; Feel love for that person. Compassion, as I have come to discover, is a silent and tender feeling that elevates one above a self-centered existence. It enables us to reside in the hearts of others, and allows us to think and feel like them. We become able to physically and emotionally situate ourselves in the place of others, becoming capable of being as they are, and feeling their agony.

Even at that age, I was sufficiently compassionate to realize that I was nothing short of an unwanted burden on my poor mother. The truth was that Ena hardly knew what to do with me, her daughter, being someone in critical need of care herself. Her life was totally bereft of the structure and form required to raise anyone. She needed raising herself, as it were. At best, Ena merely tolerated my presence in her life, having little or no choice in the matter. On my own part, realizing only too well that I was nothing but a liability on my mother, I tried all I could not to appear an unnecessary baggage. I tried to conduct myself as well, and as unobtrusively as I could. As it happened, I could see just how much danger we were both in. So, in a way I carried the psychological burden of being the one who could see just how terribly untenable our situation was. In a way, I transformed into the little adult who worried incessantly on our joint behalf. My mother appeared totally oblivious to the dangers inherent in the desperate and deplorable life she was leading, and I spent the entire time worrying incessantly about our joint safety. When you added this to the fact that I had to go to school, which was as yet uninterrupted, you had the perfect recipe for unimaginable trauma in a young girl's life. However, another unpleasant twist was just about to unfurl itself.

Gradually, the time for my examinations approached. This was the examination whose fees Grandmother Salome had been compelled to refund to Ms. Lane, my school principal, and which had resulted in my first major altercation with Salome. One day, a couple of weeks before the examination date, Ena suddenly appeared at my school. Immediately I spotted her outside the school, I knew something dramatic must be the precursor to the rare visit. I went out of my classroom to meet my mother.

"We are leaving to go and live in the country, near your grandmother. Go and get your books. We leave immediately," Ena announced flatly.

I was shocked beyond mere unbelief.

"Come on mom, you know very well that I can't go anywhere right now. My exams are barely two weeks away!"

"I am leaving this town. Are you coming? Come on, go and get your books. Let's go!" Ena countered, not looking particularly bothered by my perfectly valid protestation.

"No! I'm not coming, mom! I have exams to take. Why are you doing this?" I replied her, frantic with anxiety.

At that moment, Ena abruptly turned, and started down the school steps, and without a backward glance, turned the corner and disappeared from sight. I went back into the classroom.

I was just a child. How could I had known, in my innocence, that my mother had meant her every word about leaving? Ena left me all alone. When I returned to the tenement building after school, I discovered that my mother had picked her few ragged belongings, and left me all alone. I was more petrified than shocked at this new turn of events. What would I do now? I had nowhere to turn to. I was all alone in this world. I sank down onto the floor in the room and considered my precarious situation. Actually, in my juvenile naïveté, I had not quite believed that my mother would leave me all alone. I was merely calling her bluff at the school. What made matters worse

41

was that where my mother had apparently relocated to was very far away. One might say it was on the other side of the country, certainly a journey of not less that six hours. Dark was setting in, so I locked myself up in the room, frightened to my bones. I had to endure the darkness, because the kerosene that fueled the lamp had been exhausted. It was a restless night for me, all alone, listening to the ominous creaks of the floor boards that came from all over the building. In the morning, I went to school. This frightful trend continued for an entire week. I would wake up in the morning, and go to school, and return in the evening to an empty room, with no food to eat. On the seventh night, the landlord came banging ferociously on the door, demanding the week's outstanding rent. I was aware that the rent was payed week in, week out. Usually, my mother's current boyfriend for a particular week would pay that week's rent. But, now there was no one to pay the rent, and I was all alone. After banging the door for about ten minutes, the landlord angrily went his way, muttering obscenities under his breath.

The tenement building had many occupants. One of them was a pleasant young man who stayed all by himself in one of the rooms down the corridor from me. He was obviously aware that Ena had absconded, leaving me all alone by myself. He came calling.

```
"You are all alone by yourself. That is dangerous. Very soon,
people will know that you are alone, and that will put you in
danger. You must find somewhere more secure to stay. I wouldn't
advise you to continue to stay here. It's not safe for you."
```

He brought me some food, and gave me money to pay a week's rent. As I was going into my second week, the landlord came calling again for the week's rent. It was clear to me that my situation was becoming altogether intolerable. Life was becoming a nightmare with no light and no food, and the constant harassment of the landlord.

At about this time, I had gotten close to a friend at school. Roxanne Denobrega was in my class. She was obviously from an affluent background, as she had manners and speech that were of a greater refinement than generally seen amongst the other students. As I would later discover, Roxanne's mother had relocated to this locality, ostensibly to make a new beginning after the breakdown of her marriage. Roxanne's elitist background generated some envy amongst her peers, who saw her as someone who put up airs. Naturally, she became the brunt of cruel jokes and outright physical assault. I came from a tomboyish background, and being bolder than most, I would quickly come to the girl's rescue. Before long, I had became a guardian angel of sorts to Roxanne. Invariably, we became quite close, and I confided in her about my terrible situation. To help me, Roxanne would allow me to walk home with her, where she would go in and sneak out some food for me. This clandestine arrangement went on for three weeks. Before long, however, Roxanne's elder sister got wind of this unusual arrangement, and discovered my sad situation. Patsy, Roxanne's elder sister, with whom I would develop a very close friendship in later years, was a school teacher. Under the very convenient guise of giving me after-school lessons, Patsy would arrange for me to eat food in the house. However, even this could only serve as a brief respite. A solution would seemingly present itself in the form of a man that I recalled as the last male consort that I had associated with my mother. It had been clear that Ena was unusually close to this man, as she even visited his mother occasionally, and I would often accompany her on such visits. Finally, in utter desperation, with nowhere else to turn to, I payed the woman a visit and narrated my sorry tale to her. Little did I know that I was, wittingly or unwittingly, inaugurating a fresh phase in my tortuous odyssey.

4

Teenage Horrors

"Cruelty towards others is always also cruelty towards ourselves."
- Paul Tillich

As I mentioned at the close of the last chapter, my mother's last male consort before she performed her totally unanticipated disappearing act, was someone for whom she evidently reserved an uncommon bond of closeness and friendship, as I had occasionally accompanied her on visits to this man's mother. Feeling totally disoriented and desperate, with no obvious respite in the horizon, I grasped on what I saw as a window of opportunity, and as a last straw. With my heart literally in my mouth, I dropped in unceremoniously on the woman in a visit that I forlornly hoped might yield some assistance, in whatever form, and especially with regards to my totally precarious circumstances of accommodation and feeding. Trying all I could to organize my thoughts and sentences into a comprehensible and coherent order, I narrated my abysmally sorry tale to her. I told her that my mother had absconded from town, leaving me to fend for myself. She sat and listened to me with unexpected patience, even as she looked suitably perturbed and concerned about my sorry plight, and feigning sincere pity, she invited me to come over to live with her family.

Little did I know that I had, wittingly or unwittingly, inaugurated a fresh phase in my tortuous odyssey of agony and woes, as it did not take long for me to discover that the woman was a mere *wolf in sheep's clothing*. The reader will soon grasp the essence behind my use of this popular idiom of Biblical origin, as it is used to describe those playing a role contrary to their real character, and with whom contact is dangerous. As Aesop's classic fable tells us, a wolf, dressed in a sheep's skin blended himself in with a flock of sheep, and every day, killed one of the sheep. When the shepherd noticed this was happening, he hanged the wolf on a very tall tree. When the other shepherds asked him why he had hanged a sheep, the shepherd answered, *"The skin is that of a sheep, but the activities were those of a wolf.'* In another version, a wolf regularly came to view a flock of sheep, but never attempted to harm any of them. Eventually, the shepherd came to trust the wolf, and much to his detriment, would even occasionally leave the wolf on guard. He returned to find his flock decimated.

The woman I came to live with was a classic wolf in sheep's clothing. My arrival at my new home would mark the beginning of one of the most abusive phases of my young life. The woman had three children. They included an older son, the man who had been Ena's boyfriend, a young girl who was a couple of years younger than me, and a young boy who was a couple years older. The woman was in the vending business, and she retailed fish, oranges and vegetables to the locals. She sourced her food wares from a bigger market that was a couple of hours away by bus. Shortly after my arrival at her house, ever so insidiously, the lot gradually started to fall on me to visit this big market twice a week to source the food items. As my routine eventually evolved, I would take an 11 pm bus, which would arrive the big market at about 1 am in the early hours of the morning. I would then have to wait until about 4.30 am when the big vendors resumed business for the day. The wait itself was an ordeal all by itself as, with hundreds of dollars in my possession, I was in constant dread of being robbed. Because of this very real possibility, I would simply huddle up in one corner, unable to close my eyes, for fear of falling asleep. Quickly making my purchases at the opening of business, I would take the <u>5 am</u> bus back to my own locality. I had to cross a river to get home. So, I would, with the help of passersby, load my wares on the boat, and cross the river. On the other side, I would load the items onto a wheelbarrow, and then wheel the heavy load home. My burden of child labor, or perhaps child slavery, didn't end there for the day. Once I was back home, I would then have to load the wares into the deep freezers for cold storage. I would then hastily prepare breakfast for the woman and her daughter. It was after all these that I could even remotely think of preparing myself for school, where I had to arrive by <u>8.30 am</u>. At close of school, I would have to quickly hurry home to set up the stands and start vending the food stuffs. Although it was, not unnaturally, a rather grueling and excruciating existence, I had little or no choice in the matter, as this was the only place that provided me with a roof over my head, and which also afforded me, at the very least, fairly decent meals on daily basis.

In the meantime, as might be totally expected in a town where news spread with the rapidity of a forest wildfire, the story had started making the rounds about the little, pretty girl from Wesley's Bar who was seen laden with heavy goods two mornings of each week. This was not totally unexpected. Most of the men that I met as I disembarked from the boat that brought me across from the bus stop were those who regularly patronized my father's Bar Restaurant. It was fairly easy to recognize the little, pretty girl who was worked virtually to the bone at Wesley's Bar. Apart from making purchases for the bar, I was also required to keep the restaurant tidy, and I could be seen sweeping, cleaning and arranging benches at all hours of the day, and that was apart from keeping the exterior of the restaurant spick and span. Therefore, not only did they recognize me on my trips on the boat, but they also assisted me to push my wheelbarrow at least halfway to my guardian's house, before turning back to continue their own boat trips to their respective workplaces. Therefore, it was merely a matter of the inevitable that I quickly became the talk of the town.

My guardian's children were spoiled rotten, and did nothing around the house, especially since I was there to do all the chores. Her younger son was particularly incorrigible, and very soon added gambling to his unfortunate list of juvenile vices. One day, perhaps in a bid to source funds to fuel his gambling habit, he stole eighty dollars from his mother's business funds. Within the hour, it became obvious that money was missing. My guardian may not have been clear about who the culprit was, but she certainly knew that it couldn't have been me. That I could conceivably have stolen her money was a most unlikely possibility indeed. Here was a young girl who she entrusted with hundreds of dollars twice a week, to go to the big vendors to purchase goods, and who never for once contemplated absconding with the money. Here was a young girl who slaved away at her vending stands making sales, day in, day out, with all the money at her disposal, and never for once did it cross her mind to run off with the sales returns. How could she now possibly appropriate a mere eighty dollars to herself? Yet, my guardian, for reasons best known to her, decided to point her accusing fingers at me. It was clear that she only wanted to punish me unjustly for a crime I obviously could not have committed. My background left no latitude for juvenile delinquency. I had been raised to totally abhor stealing, lying and disrespect. The long and short of the sordid episode was that my guardian descended on me and gave her a hideous beating, and then excommunicated me from the main house.

The topography of my guardian's house was a far cry from what I had been accustomed to at my father's house. While my father's house was located on an open street that was illuminated at night by streetlights, allowing safe and secure passage for people in the darkness, my guardian's house was located in a valley, and sat isolated on its own land plot on a hillside. In that desolate terrain, only weed strewn paths connected the houses that dotted that hillside. The entire neighborhood was usually covered in dense, inky blackness at night, with no soul in sight. It was on one of such nights that my guardian expelled me from the main house and asked me to sleep outside. The fear that gripped me at this foreboding prospect can only be imagined. The home's toilet conveniences were of the outdoor type and

CHILD OF A CHILD

was located some distance from the main building. With nowhere else to lay my head for the night, I crawled into the toilet, and rolling myself up into a ball, I curled up for the night, and of course, totally terrified of the darkness, I was quite unable to sleep a wink. This would be my sleeping quarters for an entire week. Each morning, at the break of dawn, which was usually around 5 am in Guyana, I would scurry back into the main house to resume my chores of sweeping, cleaning, dusting, cooking and opening up the vending stands before hurrying up to prepare to resume school for 8.30 am. Instructively, throughout that whole week, my guardian did not as make the remotest reference to how I was coping outside the house at night, an eloquent testimony to the woman's combined insensitivity, lack of compassion and bottomless cruelty.

Over the years, I have had cause to reflect deeply on the sheer amount of cruelty I was exposed to as a child. In many respects, it has allowed me to gain a deeper understanding of human nature. Why are some people cruel to others who don't pose any threat to them, sometimes, even their own children or grandchildren? Where does this behavior come from, and what purpose does it serve? *"Humans are the glory and the scum of the universe,"* wrote the French philosopher, Blaise Pascal, in 1658. Little has changed since his days. We love and we loathe. We help and we harm. We reach out a hand and we stick in the knife. It is perfectly understandable if someone lashes out in retaliation or self-defense. But, when someone harms the harmless, we are left confounded. We typically do things to *receive pleasure* or to *avoid pain*. For most of us, hurting others causes us to feel their pain. We don't like this feeling. This suggests two reasons people may harm the harmless; either they don't feel the other person's pain, or they enjoy feeling the others' pain. Yet, another reason people may harm the harmless is because they nonetheless see a threat. Someone who doesn't imperil your body or wallet can still threaten your social status. This helps to explain otherwise puzzling actions, such as when people harm others who help them financially.

It would probably be fair to say that the majority of the people conform to our ideal of kindness and friendliness. While it might not always feel like it when you're running to work, and people are jostling and pushing you, just to get ahead of you on the train or on the bus, when it comes down to the basics, most of us are basically good. Indeed, most of us are filled with a sense of compassion and love, and become distressed whenever we see other people suffering. Every now and then, you will encounter a person who is just not nice, or someone who simply seems not to care about how you feel. Perhaps there is not even any personal gain in it for them. Maybe they are just mean and bitter. They might insult you, make your life a misery at work, be rude to you on the phone, or even commit crimes that violate your human rights. In some cases, even those people who would otherwise be kind and generous can have moments of cruelty and outbursts of violent rage. But where does this cruelty come from, and why are some people just plain mean?

As I have come to discover, while the precise reasons for meanness and cruelty vary, in the vast majority of instances you will likely find that people who are mean act that way because they have personal issues. In other words, they are unhappy themselves, and from here their mood then spreads like a virus as they are mean to other people. Many emotions can lead to you mistreating others, and if the emotions you feel are chronic and longstanding, then it will mean that you are constantly treating others poorly, while if the emotions are acute and short-lived, it will lead to short violent outbursts that seem to others to be out of character. Low self-esteem, for instance, might not technically be an '*emotion*' as such, but having a low self-esteem can cause you to lash out and take this out on others in a bid to raise your own self-esteem. Most of the time, this will easily translate to putting others down and degrading them, and the reason we do this is that we are not confident in ourselves. When someone with a low self-esteem says to someone that they look short, it makes them feel taller themselves. It is some sort of of preemptive self-defense, or a way of deflecting attention away from a perceived weakness.

We all know that anger can cause us to think irrationally. Anger causes our heart rate to increase, and it causes us to lose some of our higher order brain-functions that are to do with forward planning. This means that we lose the ability to accurately consider the outcome and consequences of our actions, because of which we blurt out insensitive pronouncements before realizing what effect this might have on the person at the receiving end. Sometimes, someone who is very angry might vent on an innocent party as a way of releasing some of the frustration they are feeling towards something they can't resolve. Additionally, if we are under a lot of stress, this causes many of the same effects as being angry, as our body triggers the fight-or-flight response. This means that we are quicker to snap and get angry, and at the same time it means that we are distracted away from what is actually occurring. This further causes us to not consider how others feel, and it means that we will be much more likely to lash out in anger.

Yet, it is not just our emotions that can cause us to do and say things that are mean or cruel. At the same time, many people can act in those ways as a result of their own misguided and maladjusted thought processes. In other words, when they are mean or unpleasant, they genuinely believe they are acting in an acceptable and logical manner. This can be a result of many different things, and is generally a faulty type of thinking. An example of this sort of faulty thinking can manifest if you are in a very competitive business environment. You might be constantly under pressure, and constantly pushing other people aside in order to get ahead. If you want to do well in business, that means keeping your eye on profits and making yourself look better than your colleagues so that you stand the best chances of promotion. At the same time, when you need results, you will have to find ways to make your staff or colleagues produce results, whether or not that means being rude and threatening. In other words, for many, the work environment is a highly dog-eat-dog world, and this can cause people to believe that is the only way to get ahead and succeed in life. Thus, their way of thinking changes, and even when they leave their work environment, they will still be trying to get ahead in any way they can. The irony is that actually doing good business is the best way to succeed, as it promotes goodwill, which will make others want to work with you.

Likewise, your personal politics and beliefs can cause you to act in a way that is perceived as cruel. For instance, if you believe that getting ahead in life is the main purpose for your existence, then this will mean that you don't think as much about how your actions will affect others. Alternatively, a person might believe in some kind of perceived hierarchy, and that gives them a sense of entitlement and superiority. This can cause them to treat others that they think are 'below' them poorly, and those people will of course see them as being cruel and unkind. There are many ways of life, and philosophies, that can promote cruelty, and sometimes people get so wrapped up in their intention to succeed in life that they eventually forget about the effect their actions have on others, or even force themselves not to think about the consequences. Again, some people simply don't have the same mechanisms for altruism and empathy that most of us do, and this can be a result of accident or of their nature. They may simply be born without the same degree of compassion as others. Such people are often defined clinically as *'psychopaths,'* and are often known to go on to commit serious crimes. Interestingly, studies also suggest that many 'high achievers' who hold positions of power and influence also meet the clinical criteria to be classed as psychopaths. I think I may have finally arrived at the conclusion that, while there are many reasons why people may act mean or cruel, the important thing to remember is that, in all these cases, the people are lashing out because of something that is *wrong* with them. If you take it personally and let it affect you, it can be highly destructive, and you might find yourself acting in a similar manner against those around you. I have learnt to let human cruelty pass over me like rivulets of water in a shower stall.

Exactly seven days into the horrendous ordeal my guardian subjected me to, I received visitors at my toilet 'bedroom.' At the quite unholy hour of 4 am, a group of young girls were returning from some nocturnal escapade or the other. They encountered the toilet in the valley, and noisily barged

51

in, in a bid to use the facility. They shockingly encountered a young girl, crouched on the floor, scared out of her wits. Not quite believing their eyes, they were stupefied into silence. As fate would have it, one of the girls was Brenda, my cousin from my father's house, who had by now graduated to fresh levels of vagrancy, and was now living an absolutely bohemian lifestyle, and totally abandoned and devoted to delinquency of the most incorrigible coloration. Shocked into silence, she informed her friends that I was her cousin. In absolute indignation, they marched to Grandmother Salome, and informing her of the undignified circumstances in which they found me, and threatened to write my father and inform him of his daughter's terrible travails. Gripped with anxiety at her inhumane treatment of me being discovered by her son, Salome hastily asked them to fetch me to her presence. Later that day at school, I received visitors. Brenda and her friends told me that my grandmother wished to see me. Salome demanded to know what had happened. After I had related my gory tale, Salome asked me to come back to live in my father's house.

Later that evening, my cruel guardian came calling. She was looking for me. Salome hid me in her bedroom during the confrontation with the woman from the valley.

"Why, hello! How may I help you? To what do I owe the honor of this rare visit?" Grandmother Salome asked her visitor, oozing patently insincere warmth and pleasantness from her every pore.

"I'm looking for Monica. She absconded from home after stealing my money. But I'm not even bothered about that. What bothers me is that her mother left her in my care, and I certainly feel some responsibility for her safety. Now, I don't even know where she is."

Grandmother Salome nodded her in supposedly silently understanding.

The woman continued speaking.

"You see, her mother suddenly decided to leave the county, and she left Monica in my care, and since then I have been taking such good care of that useless girl. She is so terrible that she even stole my eighty dollars. Now, how am I ever going to explain her disappearance to her mother when she comes calling? I mean, I still feel some sort of responsibility towards her."

Grandmother Salome looked suitably surprised.

"She was here earlier today, but stayed only an hour, claiming she was going to look for her mother, and I believe she must have left town by this time. But, come to think of it, since she is obviously a thief, why would you be anxious to have her back? Isn't this really good riddance to rubbish?"

"That may well be so, but how will I ever explain to her mother that I don't know her whereabouts?"

Salome, being every bit the tyrant herself, was perfectly willing to play the woman's game.

"Oh, I wouldn't bother so much about her, if I were you. A thief is a thief any day. She is of no useful purpose to you. At best, she will only end up stealing larger sums from you, and you wouldn't really like that, would you?"

After a few hours of talking back and forth, the woman finally left.

I was back in my father's house. But, if I felt anything had changed in my grandmother's feeling and attitude towards me, I was grossly mistaken, as very soon, the old pattern of my total subjection to a life of hard labor was re-instituted, and my life of child slavery in my own father's house resumed all over again. I was back to the old routine of sweeping, cleaning, dusting, cooking and keeping store, and then going to school. Naturally, the old cycle of intermittent beatings and excommunication onto the verandah started all over again. I will, however, have to admit that sleeping on the verandah was sheer luxury compared to my recent gruesome experience at my mother's tenement room, and my guardian's toilet exile.

Shortly after I returned to my father's house, something quite as dramatic as it was unexpected happened, and it was to drastically alter the equation of my existence in a manner no one could have possibly foreseen. Brenda, my cousin, was becoming more and more belligerent with each passing day. One day, she got into a particularly ferocious street fight. In an attempt to throw a stone brick at her adversary, the brick mistakenly hit a baby, who died instantly. Naturally, this caused a great uproar in the neighborhood, and in a twinkle of an eye, it had become a most frightening police case. Salome, totally distraught, embarked on measures to douse the ensuing tension. As happens in such situations, a solution would be found in monetary terms. Finally, Salome was able to reach an amicable settlement with all involved parties at an astronomical monetary cost, which, as events would later prove, set even Wesley's business back considerably. The immediate fallout of this was that, Brenda, who hitherto had some access to funds, was now left high and dry, with no further access to funds that were now terribly depleted by her latest misadventure. In fact, the situation became so appalling that Salome could no longer even afford to make bulk purchases of stock for the restaurant. In the circumstances, the lot now fell on me to, every other day, go across the river to buy stocks piecemeal from the major dealers, and I would often have to buy cigarettes in cartons on such trips. Therefore, it became a routine for me to walk up to the restaurant workers every two days to ask for money to make purchases of this sort for the restaurant. This was the arrangement that Brenda saw fit to expediently exploit, and which inadvertently set me up for my next adventure in teenage drama.

Brenda walked up to me.

"Mother's maltreatment of you is getting worse by the day. You can't go on like this. What are you going to do about it?"

Salome was referred to as 'mother' by everyone in Linden, inclusive of her own grandchildren. It was also true that, at this time, I was at my tether's end with regards to the horrible suffering I was painfully enduring at my grandmother's hands. I was now in a position to appreciate the apprehension that Grandmother Virginia Subryan had expressed when I had refused to follow her back to Berbice at the end of my second vacation at my father's house. I was now, quite understandably, perfectly willing to go back to my maternal grandmother, secure in the belief that I would live the semblance of a normal and decent life with her. This was the situation that Brenda was now trying to help me exploit.

"You can't go on like this, Monica. You've got to do something before you come to some harm or the other. This is what I want you to do. Go to the restaurant. Tell them you need twenty dollars to go and buy some cigarettes. They will give you the money. Then, I will use the money and take you to Georgetown, where my boyfriend is. Together, while in Georgetown, we will find away to locate your other grandmother, and put a stop to your suffering."

Naturally, this was music to my willing ears. I was fed up. Life was too harrowing to bear any longer. Of course, getting the twenty dollars proved infinitely easy, as I did this frequently for purchase purposes. With the money in my hands, Brenda took me out of the house, and we took a bus to Georgetown, and to yet another phase in my season of accelerated growth to precocious adulthood.

5

The Juvenile Prisoner

"The last place I would ever want to go is prison." - Martha
Stewart

What I would easily consider my first and rare act of rebellion was encouraged by my cousin, Brenda, the eldest of the four children that my deceased aunt left for my grandmother, Salome, to raise, an assignment to which she devoted so much passion and commitment that she even concocted the combined notion and ambition that, against any and every imaginable odd, those children would inherit my father's estate and legacy. As it happened, the only real and potent threat to her scheming and machinations was my rather unwelcome and inconvenient presence in their lives, motivating her to subject me to the most horrendous coloration of childhood slavery anyone could possibly visit on a juvenile. Brenda herself, a monument to adolescent delinquency and totally maverick vagrancy, having put herself in the perfectly untenable position of somehow getting involved in a street brawl that led to the untimely death of a young child, that unfortunate incident leading to the deployment of a humongous sum of money from my father's restaurant and bar business, found herself in rather desperate financial straits, as there was now virtually no business funds to either pilfer, or squeeze out of our grandmother. As it were, the huge sums that were payed out as compensation to the victim's family and law enforcement had all but wiped out both the working capital and recurrent profits of my father's business. In fact, the business now ran on the daily ad hoc basis of retail purchase of even cigarettes for sale at the bar, a prospect that was not so daunting since the customers were perfectly willing to provide the little sums of money required for such emergency purchases.

Brenda, to the eternal credit of her mischievously ingenious mind, quickly saw an opportunity to exploit, both my terrible ordeal at the hands of our grandmother, and our hapless dependence on our customers for the meager sums needed for the emergency purchase of items for the bar. She needed cash desperately, and was willing to extort it by the easiest means available, and by so doing, offering me a ray of hope for escaping Grandmother Salome's tyranny. She asked me to go to the restaurant and ask the customers for twenty dollars to go and buy some cigarettes. On the perfectly valid assumption that the money would be freely given, her plan was to use the money to take me to Georgetown, where her boyfriend was. Together, while in Georgetown, we would find a way for me to return to Grandmother Subryan, my maternal grandmother, at Berbice, so that my suffering could finally come to an end. This was music to my ears. I was already at my tether's end with a life that was increasingly becoming too harrowing and nightmarish to bear, and the looming prospect of being in the company of people who actually cared about me was something I simply could not resist. Naturally, getting the twenty dollars was easy enough. With the money in our possession, Brenda and I took a bus to Georgetown to commence the next inglorious phase of my accelerated growth to precocious adulthood.

Georgetown is the capital and largest city of Guyana. Nicknamed the *"Garden City of the Caribbean,"* it is the administrative and financial centre of the country, and the city is at the center of Guyana's economy. All the executive departments of Guyana's government are located in the city, including Parliament Building, Guyana's Legislative Building and the Court of Appeals,

Guyana's highest judicial court. The State House, the official residence of the head of state, as well as the offices and residence of the head of government, are both located in Georgetown. CARICOM headquarters is also based in Georgetown. Georgetown is also famous for its British colonial architecture, including the tall painted-timber St George's Cathedral and the iconic Stabroek Market. The city of Georgetown began as a small town in the 18th century, and it was the French who made it a capital city when they colonized it in 1782. Georgetown was originally called Longchamps by the French, but when the town was restored to the Dutch in 1784, it was renamed Stabroek, and finally renamed Georgetown on April 29, 1812 in honor of King George III of England. The names of Georgetown's streets reflect the influence of the Dutch, French and English who administered the town at different periods of its history.

So, it was to this sprawling metropolis that Brenda took me when we absconded from my father's house. The bus journey to Georgetown took approximately two hours, within which time Grandmother Salome had gotten wind of our infamous expedition, and had promptly contacted the police to intercept us, not necessarily because she was overly concerned about my safety, but more because she wanted to avoid having to explain my whereabouts to my father when he returned. Finding Georgetown an exciting and bustling city, the entire adventure was by now becoming quite appealing to me, especially since Brenda was obviously inclined to both proudly demonstrate her sophistication by her familiarity with the big city, and show me off as her nice-looking cousin. Eventually, we arrived at our final destination, Brenda's boyfriend's mother's house, who received us warmly. Dropping our luggage, we went off to see the town. Brenda took me to the market, where in total fascinating with the unaccustomed sea of faces and sights, I simply couldn't help experiencing a certain thrill and excitement. I also felt so distractedly elated, and perhaps, in a strange way, happy. Yet, even now, I can't quite say if I was happy because of the prospect of returning to Berbice, or because I had finally escaped the horrors of Linden, a town for which I reposed only memories of horrendous abuse, or simply because of my sudden introduction to such an exciting and vibrant city. When we got back to the house, we were informed that the police were looking for us. Under the totally misguided belief that Grandmother Subryan was already looking for me, I went straight to Bricktown police precinct, the main police station in Georgetown. Literally palpitating with excitement that I was going to reconnect with my grandmother, my shock can only be imagined when I was promptly detained by the police. I was informed that Grandmother Salome had called that she was on her way to retrieve me back home, as I was underage, and she had given the police specific and unambiguous instructions that I should be held captive until her arrival.

Bricktown police station was hell on Earth. Most certainly, it was not designed to incarcerate the underaged. I was definitely underage. I initially spent all of two days in an absolutely terrifying environment. Against the glaring backdrop of a total lack of law enforcement professionalism, I was installed in a holding cell occupied by adult women who had committed the worst possible crimes, such as murder, prostitution and robbery. All the women in that cell were adults, except me. The cell itself was constructed of concrete, and it flooded whenever it rained, which was quite often. That meant half of the cell was literally flooded with water, while the other half hosted just one bunk bed, a territory that was the goal of ferocious fighting for space, with the loudest and most aggressive person prevailing to dominate the top of the bunk, while the others hunkered down at the bottom of the bunk. The cell was pitch dark, and light filtered in only from a little hole that was way up, close to the ceiling. Every morning, the jingling of keys announced a breakfast that was little more than tepid warm water that had been colored, rather than enriched, with a little milk and sugar. Lunch was invariably some rice with a little bit of gravy, while dinner was celebrated with bread and tea. No one bothered to come into the cell to monitor what was going on inside. All interaction with our jailers began and ended at the cell door.

I had not committed any crime. My name was certainly not listed on any crime docket. Therefore, there simply wasn't any reason for my unjust incarceration. As a matter of fact, no one at the police station could even remotely offer any cogent reason for my presence there. I simply remained behind lock and key, with my only interaction with the outside world constrained to the appearance of my jailers at the cell door, even as the other women, one after the other, were let out to go and make appearances at the courts. I would remain in hapless confinement for over five months, with a seemingly endless line of female criminals coming and going from that cell. I was locked up in a women's prison having done nothing wrong, and committed no crime. I was in that intolerable state of affairs just because the system failed me. I was there just because the adults in my life had malevolently failed me. Grandmother Salome's antipathy for me was obviously now at its extreme, as she made it abundantly clear to the police that she wanted me behind bars, and to rot away behind those bars, at her pleasure.

At some point, I simply became mute. I stopped talking. I stopped responding to human communication. Yet, some respite came my way in the form of the *de facto* leader of the cell, what one might refer to, in crude parlance, as the *baddest* woman in the cell. I think she was probably drawn to me because, despite the untenable situation in which I unwittingly found myself, I remained both respectful and helpful. The woman started to take a more than mere cursory interest in me. She ensured that I had a comfortable place to lay down my head and sleep. She made sure that I got my share of whatever miserable food that was served. This was a woman who was in custody because she had committed murder. She was said to have killed a man who had serially abused her.

One day, she made a court appearance. The judge asked her if she had anything to say. This woman told the judge that an innocent young girl was locked up in the cell, and that there seemed to be no one who cared about her. Worse, she told the judge, the young girl had no reason on Earth to be locked up in a cell. She pleaded with the judge to investigate my matter. Apparently, the judge took her story seriously, because a social worker suddenly appeared, and I was brought out of the cell and taken to an office, where I stayed for two more days during which they could not get any information out of me. I remained mute. They didn't know who I was. They didn't know where I came from. There was no documentation whatsoever about me. On the third day I broke down crying, and finally gave them all the information at my disposal about my grandmother. I told them about everything that had happened to me up to that point, and they contacted Grandmother Subryan in Berbice.

What happened next was totally unexpected. My mother suddenly materialized at the police station. She had come to fetch me. Naturally, I was relieved. I was relieved because I thought I was now finally on my way back to Berbice and the maternal grandmother who was guaranteed to offer me the security that I now so much craved. As matters later turned out, however, not only was I both terribly mistaken and misguided, I was actually about to embark on another roller coaster of traumatic events that would irrevocably alter the trajectory of my young life, and in ways that I couldn't have ever imagined.

My mother arrived the prison late one afternoon. What I initially thought was the first leg of our journey to Berbice was to the home of a lady my mother introduced to me as my godmother. To my utter surprise, the journey, at least my own journey, ended at that woman's house. Her house was about half an hour away from the police precinct where I'd been incarcerated for all of five months. My mother summarily announced that I would be staying with the lady until she came back for me. Instantly, I felt an ominous sense of foreboding. I had a terrible feeling of *déjà vu*. I had been along this road before. My mother did not disappoint me. She never came back. Once again, she left me to my own unfortunate fate, high and dry.

I ended up the perfectly unwilling guest of the woman. Popularly acknowledged to be an obeah in that part of town, she inspired holy fear in everyone, including even the police. Clearly, a fresh round of nightmare had just been inaugurated in my life, as not only my domestic circumstances were currently much less than salutary, the environment itself was nothing short of the abominable. This obeah woman lived in the very decrepit part of town, where the human traffic, on daily basis, comprised of the dregs of the city, mainly undesirable elements on the wrong side of the law. It was also what might be easily termed, the "rough side of town," being populated by all manner of miscreants. The entire neighborhood was afflicted with a mixture of a high crime rate, poor sanitation, and rough accommodation. The houses were little more than tiny little shacks, and travel on roads that could only be described as muddy paths was a total nightmare. The long and short of my pathetic story was that I simply reverted to my, shall I say, accustomed role as a child slave. I had to embark on frequent trips to the market. I had to cook. I had to clean the house. I had to wash her clothes. Naturally, all thought of school was all but forgotten. To compensate for my lack of schooling, I resorted to clandestine reading when she was not looking. I had virtually no time to myself, and if she caught me reading, an activity she considered almost a mortal sin, I received the beating of my life. All that was demanded of me was work, work and more work.

It was was on one of those forays into the market to buy groceries for cooking that the events that would have such a cataclysmic impact on my life started. As I was walking to the market, a man on a motorcycle rode past me. Unexpectedly, he stopped, and asked me if I wasn't Brenda's cousin. That was when my memory was sufficiently jogged to remember that I had seen this man on the first day that I came to Georgetown, at Brenda's boyfriend house. Apparently, he was a friend to Brenda's boyfriend. He had been briefly introduced to me as Cliff Halley. I explained all that had happened to me since our first meeting. I explained how I had reported at the police precinct in the mistaken belief that I was going to reconnect with my maternal grandmother at Berbice, only to end up in unholy incarceration for all of nearly six months. When my mother finally came to take charge of me, it was only to drop me off at this lady's house, marking the beginning of a tenure of slavery. Naturally, he knew exactly who the lady was. Everyone knew the lady. Everyone was mortally afraid of the lady. I accepted his gracious offer of a ride to the market, where I bought the groceries, and then he took me back home. The next day, I ran into him again on my way to the market. On this occasion, he offered to come everyday to transport me to the market. Not unnaturally, I was overwhelmed with excitement, as this was virtually the only person I was familiar with in the entire neighborhood, and it somehow seemed very much like being around family once again. As this turn of events made me extremely happy, my harrowing days became somewhat more bearable, as I now even looked forward to going to the market, just so as to have the opportunity to talk to the man. Cliff was extremely nice to me. In fact, after the second week of giving me rides, back and forth to the market, and learning more about my untenable situation, he started giving me money. Naturally, there was no way I could spend the money. If the obeah woman found out that I had money, I would be extremely hard put to explain its source, and that would mean hell on Earth for me. In the event, I hid the money, and started saving it.

Cliff Haley was a soldier at that time, and he made it clear that he was not afraid of the obeah woman. The more he gained familiarity with my unfortunate circumstances in the woman's house, the more convinced he seemed to become to help me in some way or the other. Finally, he said he would come and talk to the woman, and ask her what exactly was going on. At first, in alarm, I baulked at the very idea. I was convinced that the woman would react in a very negative manner. But Cliff managed to convince me that my life would become infinitely better if I agreed to his suggestion. He did come on a visit to the woman. The long and short of his intervention was that he told the lady that he would periodically give her money for my upkeep. The woman readily agreed to his suggestion, as she even seemed to take a liking to him, allowing him to freely visit her house. However, on these visits, I was never allowed to be privy to their conversations. It was, however, also becoming rather evident that the woman was fast developing intentions for Cliff that clearly bordered on the romantic. This was obviously not a welcome development for me, as she now saw me as an obstacle in her path to win Cliff's amorous attention, whom she was much older than, while Cliff himself was much older than me. Life went on in this uneasy manner for quite some time. Cliff would bring me books, so I could read. I was given a bit of latitude to take lunch to Cliff, and I would use that time to read. In the event, I was also beginning to be explicably drawn to Cliff, if only because he was the only person who seemed to care about me. He gave me money on a regular basis, and spent quality time with me everyday in his valiant attempt to make my presence in the woman's home less harrowing. On her own part, the woman treated me with a little bit more consideration, yet I could sense trouble in the horizon, since her intentions towards Cliff were of a distinct romantic flavor. Matters, however, would take a paradoxic turn for the unexpected, as Cliff, on his own part, was on the verge of introducing an entirely new and surprising dimension to his relationship with me, and things would never quite be the same again for me.

6

Teenage Pregnancy

"What the daughter does, the mother did." - Jewish Proverb

As I mentioned in the previous chapter, Cliff Halley was tremendously good to me. Yet, ever so surreptitiously, and ever so subtly, he started to exert a certain pressure on his relationship with me. At the beginning, his attention appeared innocent and benign enough for me to attribute it to sheer human kindness and compassion. Much later, a certain subtle aggressiveness crept into the picture. Naturally, he became progressively brazen. In between, it became clear that his strategy was to employ his kindness and consideration as a tool to make me feel guilty, such that I might be compelled to reciprocate his magnanimity by offering certain favors which initially appeared unclear to me. To state that I became increasingly bewildered would be to put my difficult position mildly. It was, however, quite clear that Cliff was starting to make me feel indebted to him in some way or the other. That was when I started to ponder a bit on what his ultimate motivation might be for being so nice to me.

Yet, it would be untrue to say I did not entirely have a clue as to his intention. While I was by no means a veteran like my cousin, Brenda, I was old enough

65

to hazard a near-accurate guess as to what a full grown man might seek from an attractive young girl. Most certainly, I had received sufficient knowledge in that department from observing all that transpired between my mother and the men that were attracted to her beauty. Even at that tender age, I was well aware that not a single one of those men cared about her. They wanted only one thing from her, and that was to sleep with her. Up till this time, despite all the physical and emotional abuse I had suffered, I had been spared the rather commonplace tragedy of rape, which was a miracle all by itself, nor had I engaged in consensual sex. Admittedly, I had been *fingered*, as they say. I had been touched inappropriately several times. My breasts and bottom had been groped, and even my private parts had been touched at some point, but I had never had penetrative sex.

Again, in keeping faith with my resolve to, as much as is within my power, use the pages of this book to touch on those life issues that directly impact a young person, I will employ my own inadvertent misadventure into early adolescent sex to highlight those dynamics that I wasn't aware of by the time I came under pressure from Cliff Halley. Adolescent sexuality is a stage of human development in which adolescents experience and explore sexual feelings. Interest in sexuality intensifies during the onset of puberty, and sexuality is often a vital aspect of a teenager's life. Sexual interest may be expressed in a number of ways, such as flirting, kissing, masturbation, or having sex with a partner. Sexual interest among adolescents, as among adults, can vary greatly, and is influenced by cultural norms, sex education, social constraints, and age-of-consent laws. Sexual activity, in general, is associated with various risks, and this is heightened by the unfamiliar excitement of sexual arousal, the attention connected to being sexually attractive, and the new level of physical intimacy and psychological vulnerability created by sexual encounters. Naturally, the risks of sexual intercourse include unwanted pregnancy and sexually transmitted diseases. These risks are much higher for young adolescents because their brains are not yet neurally mature. Several parts of the brain that are deemed important for self-control, delayed gratification, risk analysis, and appreciation are not yet fully mature, and are usually not fully developed until the early 20s. Partially, because of this, young adolescents are generally less equipped than adults to make sound decisions and anticipate consequences of sexual behavior.

Until their first act of sexual intercourse, adolescents generally see virginity in one of the following ways; as a gift, a stigma, or a normal step in development. Girls typically think of virginity as a gift, while boys think of virginity as a stigma. Girls tend to view giving someone their virginity in the light of offering it as a very special gift. Because of this, they often expect something in return, such as heightened emotional intimacy with their partners. Yet, most female adolescents often end up feeling both disappointed and disempowered because they often do not believe they actually received what they expected in return. They feel they have given something up, and do not feel the offer of a gift was appreciated. Thinking of virginity as a stigma often disempowers males because they feel deeply ashamed, and often try to hide the fact that they were virgins from their partners which, for some, results in their partners teasing them and criticizing them about their limited sexual experience. The girls who view virginity as a stigma tend not to experience this shaming. Even though they privately think of virginity as a stigma, girls generally believe that society values their virginity because of the stereotype that women are sexually passive. This makes it easier for them to lose their virginity once they decide to do so, because they feel society has a more positive view on female virgins, even rendering them more sexually attractive.

There are many reasons why adolescents indulge in sexual activity. Fundamentally, they like the way it feels. The human body has thousands of touch receptors. While there are many factors that can cause sex to feel good, suffice it to say that sex can be a very pleasurable physical and emotional experience and there shouldn't be an attempt to conceal this fact from adolescents. We might prefer that the "feel good receptors" come alive only at the very time when someone makes a marital commitment. The truth is more prosaic than that. Those receptors come alive even in childhood, and puberty itself brings about even stronger sensations. There is simply no denying the fact that sex and all types of loving physical intimacy were created for pleasure and enjoyment. When people in uncommitted relationships engage in this type of relationship, it often feels good, and it is only later that the consequences are felt. Yet, not everyone recognizes that the things they are struggling with later in life are connected to this early sexual conflicts. There are many pleasurable experiences and sensations in life, and some are meant to be experienced at different times than others. A teenager might be thrilled to begin driving. Their parents might even let them try driving in some remote location. This does not mean they should begin driving at this point in their life.

Peer pressure is significant in early experience of sexual activity. Even when a girl doesn't want to have sex, she may give in to pressure for fear of the other person leaving her, or rejecting her. Many adolescents feel a lot of pressure to "fit in." There is a very clear message that it matters whether or not they have "had sex." As we easily learn from news items, bullying and being bullied is real. Cyber bullying, verbal bullying, school bullying, text bullying, and physical bullying can be extremely difficult for adolescents to endure. In fact, we may not admit it, but parents can also feel pressure from their peers that, "Everyone is doing it. We have to accept that times have changed and they are going to do it anyway." There is also pressure from the culture. Sex sells! It is true. Pornography, fashion, TV commercials, and movies all make sex a huge commodity, and many industries are capitalizing on it. No matter where you turn, you can hardly avoid seeing more *skin* than you intended to see, with church, honors classes and chorus recitals being no exception. This crosses all classes, and all types of people. When teenagers are bombarded with images and messages, their sense of "normal" simply cannot be expected to remain normal. They begin to see everything as relative to the culture that they are exposed to. They might have once dreamed of being a wife and mother, and may still dream of that, but today, *normal* seems to have become one girl *'making out'* with another girl in the hotel pool on a class trip, after popping a few pills or having a few drinks. Although the myth of "everyone is doing it" is still a myth, people are accepting it as truth everyday.

Sometimes, adolescents feel self-defeated because of abusive or previous choices. When they feel like they have already given up their "first time," they may feel like there is no point in abstaining any longer. Some young people who have been raped or molested feel this defeat as well. Additionally, most young people do not really understand what love is. Love is a feeling and a commitment. The feeling of love ebbs and flows. While boyfriends and girlfriends can "feel" love today, tomorrow they might feel something else. This is true in marriage as well. A commitment does not depend on the feeling of the day. Sex might make you feel "in love," but it doesn't actually situate you in a "committed relationship." In a committed relationship, sex is a beautiful act of love. Rebellion can also play a part in adolescent sexuality. Rebellion has at least three root possibilities. The first is our inclination to do what we shouldn't do, just because we can and we want to. The second is a reaction to a poor relationship within the immediate family, either between an adolescent and one or both parents, or a poor relationship between the parents, while the third might be from something as relatively simple as a temporary anger at a parent, leading to a teenager acting impulsively.

Curiosity is also a significant factor. Adolescents wonder. They are curious. They may be curious about how alcohol tastes and makes them feel. People are curious and some people act on their curiosity without first considering the consequences. Drugs and alcohol are mind altering substances that lower one's inhibition. An adolescent is more likely to do much more than she intended at a party, or on a date situation, if she is under the influence of a substance. Even more frightening, others can facilitate an adolescent to become either drug or alcohol intoxicated in order to sexually assault her much more easily, and with much less chance of being reported. The drugged person may not even be conscious enough to know what is happening to them, or who is doing it to them.

Adolescents use sex to express love, and to receive love. Teenagers need connection. Young children often crave physical touch, and parents love to give it. As they grow up, it tends to become less and less. Teenagers may be pulling away from parents and clinging to peers. There may be a great deal of love in the home, but sometimes teenagers cannot receive it. There may be a great deal of stress in the home, which crowds out the feeling of love. Of equal impact is the phenomenon of *pseudo-maturity*, or *false maturity*. Some adolescents feel set apart from their peers. They view themselves as "more mature" than their peers. They may be connected with older people who are impressed by their "maturity," and want to support them. They may have an "open and accepting" view of their body, in which anything that feels good is good, and should be enjoyed as often as one wishes. If girl-girl touching feels good, they do it. If boy-girl touching feels good, they do it. If watching pornography feels good, they do it. If touching with different people feels good, they do it. Some of such "pseudo matures" are involved in sexual relationships with much older men or women, some even with their parents' consent because they so deeply want to believe that their child is really that mature. In fact, one has heard of parents who say, "I know she is young, but she is very mature. I am okay with the sex, I just want to make sure she is fine." Naturally, this also means many parents are not taking a sufficiently strong stand. Despite the current-day philosophy that so many have adopted, children and teenagers cannot be left to decide every important thing on their own, without sound guidance from a trusted adult. Seeds will be sown in the hearts and mind of our youth. If we leave that to the culture, who knows where our children will end up? Teenagers report overwhelmingly that they base important decisions on, at least, a consideration of the morals, values and opinions of their parents. This leads us seamlessly into the fact that adults often fail to uphold the moral standard that they expect from their children. When parents are unwilling to get out of their seat and turn off the TV, or say "no" to an inappropriate movie, or say "no" to a revealing outfit, how can one expect their children to say "no" to such things? Parents definitely have an influence on their children, and they ought to own that responsibility. They shouldn't give it over to the school teacher, or to the TV, or to friends and other families.

In my own case, the significant factor in my evolving sexual relationship with Cliff Halley was the unbearable pressure he mounted on me. Curiously, I finally resolved in my mind that I would allow him have sex with me. Yet, it was patently clear that I was not really aware of the dynamics involved in a sexual relationship. Although I was unaware of exactly what sex was, I agreed to go with him and have sex. As matters turned out, I almost immediately became pregnant with my wonderful son, Paul. Yet, the ensuing journey, as all the other journeys I had embarked upon so far, was not a particularly pleasant one. Shortly after our sexual encounter, Cliff came over to tell my guardian, the lady obeah, about it. He told the lady that I was pregnant. Of course, I hadn't a clue what he was talking about. How could I be pregnant after a single sexual encounter? I had no experience, and I had no role model or mentor to guide me and educate me. As it turned out, I was, indeed, pregnant. The woman's reaction can only be imagined. She went absolutely berserk. She was beside herself with self-righteous rage. After giving me the beating of my life, she threw me, and everything I had, out in the rain and the mud. I had no choice than to run to Cliff. Clearly, that was his intention all along. Most certainly, it is difficult to fathom that, in divulging the information to my guardian that he had impregnated me, he did not fully expect that she would instantly excommunicate me. I guess he gave her the news, and simply went back home to calmly and patiently await the expected aftermath. His prediction was absolutely accurate. I finally arrived his doorstep.

I ended up coming to live with Cliff, his father and his stepmother in Georgetown, on a street called Princess Street. Cliff's parents were very nice to me, and they, more or less, treated me as my grandmother in Berbice treated me. I felt loved and wanted. I felt like I was finally with family. Finally, I seemed to have found people who treated me as a human being, and who treated me like family. I was happy. Yet, this happiness would not last very long as a new and ugly challenge soon reared its head.

I had not been introduced to sex in a loving manner. Sex had merely been a convenient way to pay a debt that I was convinced I had to pay. Now that I was living with Cliff, it soon became clear that he expected me to continue to pay that debt on daily basis. My debt had suddenly become a cross to bear, and an unbearable albatross around my neck. The man wanted sex everyday. He wanted it in the morning. He wanted it for lunch. He wanted it at bedtime. He was simply insatiable. What he didn't reckon with was that I was having none of his sexual gluttony. I simply wasn't prepared to be a receptacle for his unbridled sexual appetite. As far as I was concerned, I was through with paying my debt to him. I was no longer prepared to be taken advantage of. Finally reconciling myself to the fact that I was pregnant, I decided to firmly draw a line in the sand. I resolved to find my way back to my grandmother at Berbice, one way or the other, and that was what I did.

Eventually, I did find myself back in Berbice, the one place I truly considered home, and my supposedly indisputable comfort zone. I told Grandmother Subryan all that had happened to me from the time she left me, walking down those steps at my father's house, crying. I told her how sorry I was not to have believed what she had predicted would be my fate, and I begged for her forgiveness. I told her how much I had suffered, and how much I wanted to be back with her. She hugged me tightly, and cried with me. She told me that she knew exactly what was going to happen to me, and that she tried so hard to convince me, but I wouldn't listen.

Then, I dropped the bombshell. I told her that I was pregnant. I also told her why I had to come back to her. I told her that I could no longer continue having sex with the father of my baby, and that all I wanted now was to stay back here with my family, and have my baby. I wanted to get back to where I was with her, with no thought of ever leaving her again. Yet, if wishes were horses, beggars would surely ride. One day, not long after my return to Berbice, Cliff suddenly turned up at the house. Matters suddenly became complicated all over again. Cliff's spirited efforts to find me finally paid off, and he tracked me down to my grandmother's house at Berbice. The interesting thing was that, my mother, very much in need of comfort too, was also back at Berbice. Clearly, we both needed the solace that Grandmother Subryan could offer. The only difference was that my mother was not living with my grandmother, but lived a mere walking distance away. When Cliff arrived at Berbice, he was very strategic in his campaign to get me back to him. He approached both my grandmother and mother, and told them how much he loved me, and wanted to marry me. He told them just how excited he was that I was having his baby, and how he wanted me to come back and raise a beautiful family with him. He related how he had treated me nicely, and with consideration while I was with him. Naturally, to grease his entreaties, he gave my grandmother some money in his bid to cajole her to encourage me to get married to him. Cliff's strategy worked perfectly. In fact, his strategy was so effective that Grandmother Subryan went as far as threatening that if I refused to marry Cliff, I might as well forget about ever speaking with her again. Basically, what my grandmother was doing was giving me an ultimatum to either get married, or get out of her house. My principal preoccupation was that if I got married to this man, I would be under the agonizing obligation of having sex with Cliff everyday.

The prospect of daily sex with Cliff was simply one I was not willing to entertain. I stood my ground that it simply wasn't going to happen. It broke my heart to see my grandmother walk away from me. Yet, what I apparently failed to understand at that time was that she was still trying to protect me. She felt that marriage would provide me a protective shelter from the world. She was also understandably worried about me having a child out of wedlock at such a tender age. Those were the reasons why she was trying so hard to push me into a marriage that I simply didn't want. I was painfully young. I did not understand her motives, and since I was abysmally lacking in experience, I did not know the enormity of what I was getting into. There was no way I could see the dangers that lay ahead of me. I had already been through so much trauma, so much hurt, so much betrayal, and so much abuse, that I was now numb. I did not think I could suffer any more than I had already endured, and so I held my ground. Remaining so resolute was not an easy task, as he had gotten both my grandmother and mother to his side through sound arguments and monetary inducement. Furthermore, he sustained the pressure by visiting often, bearing gifts and money. Eventually, the pressure from both my grandmother and mother became unbearable. My grandmother stopped talking to me entirely. In the unfortunate circumstances, I was compelled to move in, once again, with my mother, who was living with a man, and the abuse started all over again.

Cliff remained unrelenting in his pressure on my mother to get me to marry him. As I remained unyielding, and to push me to act against my own will, the domestic abuse started all over again. I recall a particularly terrible day. My mother had tried to engage me in an argument. I remained mute, refusing to respond to her provocation. In total frustration, she boiled some water, and attempted to throw it on me. Luckily, not much of it got onto me. This made her even angrier, and she assaulted me physically. That particular incident drove me to a breakdown of sorts, and I started walking on the street, until I arrived at a famous landmark in Berbice called Canje Bridge. I found my way to the middle of that bridge. Later, I would be given the details of what occurred on that bridge, and on that fateful day. However, there was absolutely no doubt that I was under a severe state of acute dysfunction, and one in which I became suicidal in both thought and deed. To express matters in very stark terms, my mind finally snapped, and simply not being able to endure further trauma, I subconsciously decided to terminate my abject suffering by ending my own life. Operating very much like a remotely-controlled zombie, my intention was to jump off the bridge. I was told that my mother was on one side of the bridge trying to get to me, while a neighbor who had just closed from work at a mental hospital where he was a registered nurse, was on the other side of the bridge. I was told that my mother could not reach me because I threatened that if she got any closer, I would jump off the bridge. In the circumstances, all she could helplessly do was cry hysterically, begging me not to do it, while asking the neighbor approaching from the other side of the bridge to help. As it happened, the neighbor was able to reach me, and perhaps drawing on his experience as a mental nurse, was able to talk me into leaving the bridge. He brought me back home to his house. He sedated me so that I could get adequate rest. He lived in the same building with us. Interestingly, it was a building that my mother and I had lived in previously, and my mother lived fairly close to him. When I woke up the next day, I was told my mother wanted to see me. I said that I wanted nothing to do with her, and that if she as much as made any attempt to see me, I would kill myself, so she stayed away from me. I remained with the neighbor, and he showed me kindness, nurturing me to a place of self sufficiency. To make myself useful, I remained at home raising chickens that laid eggs which I sold, apart from other forms of petty trading. In that manner, without venturing out of that safe place, I was able to make some money. The kind neighbor would take out my goods and sell them for me, and in that way, I was able to save money with which I would take care of the baby I was expecting.

The neighbor's name was Cecil Levine. He treated me like a princess. Not once did he make an inappropriate advance towards me. He never attempted to sexually assault me, and never did he abuse me physically. He was always respectful and kind towards me. Rather, he devoted time to counseling and advising me. He taught me how to set up my little business. He taught me how to make money, and how to save that money. He brought me a lot of books to read, and got me back on the road of honoring and honing my intellect. When I went into hospital to have my baby, I was still living at Cecil's house. My baby was premature because of the stress I had gone through, and shortly after the baby's birth, I became quite ill. Additionally, I was totally ignorant of the procedures that attend the birth of a baby. In fact, Cecil, who was there with me every step of the way, had to sign his name onto the baby's birth certificate, and took care of every other aspect of the process. A few days later, I was discharged from hospital. I came back home to hold my baby, even as Cecil Levine remained the nicest, the most caring, and the most loving person to me and my son. I find myself eternally grateful to this wonderful man for talking me off that bridge, and for making himself available as an invaluable support system at that very critical phase of my tumultuous life.

A couple of months after my son was born, my mother, who had remained implacably in love with my father, showed up with the same old request for me to visit my father. Naturally, I bluntly refused. Instead, I penned a nine-page letter for her to deliver to my father, and in which I sought to irrevocably sever all connection with him, describing in graphic detail all the horrible elements of my trip to hell and back several times, all because of him. My mother tried everything under the sun to get me to pay him a visit, but I remained adamant in my resolve not to do so. It was Cecil Levine who finally talked me into going to see my father. His argument was unassailable. In his words, "If there is the slightest possibility that you can give your son a life much better than the one you have lived, it is worth taking that opportunity, just to give your child a chance to have a better life than you have had." That was how I ended up going back to see my father. I wanted to give my son hope. I wanted to put the world at his feet. I wanted him to have endless possibilities to choose from.

7

My Mother

"Mothers hold their children's hands for a short while, but their hearts forever." - Nitya Prakash

I distinctly recall the first time I set eyes on the woman who gave birth to me. In the realm of a child's fantasy world, she looked like a movie star. She was uncommonly beautiful and elegant-looking in my juvenile vision. I was living at the house in Berbice, with my grandmother and six uncles, all of whom I thought were my biological brothers. Although we all existed in that house on the very margins of severe material deprivation, our extreme poverty did not stop me from seeing Grandmother Subryan as my mother, this house as my true home, and this good people as my family. This was where I belonged. This was everything my life was all about. Then, suddenly, this beautiful woman materialized from seemingly nowhere to shatter all that blissful myth.

She came visiting, and declared to me in unequivocal terms that she was my mother, and that I would be going to live with her. I was under no illusion as to how I felt at that epochal instant. The feeling that coursed through my little body was such a wonderful one that, even now, words fail me in my attempt to describe it. Most certainly, it was a mixture of exhilaration, elation and pride. To say that I was so happy that such a beautiful woman was my mother would be putting it mildly. To cut a long story short, that was how my mother, the fairy tale princess, came to take me away from my Grandmother Queen, to go and live with her. I would be leaving my grandmother, the queen, for the very first time. My mother was the quintessential mom. She had come with pretty dresses, and ribbons for my hair. All dressed up, and preening like the prettiest peacock ever, I joined my mother to take a ferry. On the voyage, she gave me ice cream, candy and chips. I was in the ninth cloud of ecstasy. To my near-heart stopping delight, this wonderful woman kept hugging and kissing me. I felt so loved that my entire young life came to a standstill, just to continue to savor the moment. Then, we disembarked from the ferry, and got into a car for the long trip to Georgetown.

Our destination was a beautiful home where my mother lived with her baby's father, a prominent man who was finance minister in the Guyanese government. He had seen her and fallen in love with her. She ended up having a baby for him. In the circumstances, she was now part of a beautiful home that had everything one could ever wish for. Clearly, my mother had arrived at the unquestionable belief that she was now in a position to take adequate care of me and her new baby. She obviously believed she could now pick up the pieces of her life, while comfortably situating her two girls in this perfect, little fairy tale life that she had conjured in her imagination. Yet, if wishes were horses, beggars would ride. The idyllic domestic setting she wished for simply did not materialize. The setting was perfect. The house was a perfect mansion. My mother was the perfect, beautiful woman of the house. My beautiful baby sister was the perfect second child of my perfect mother. My stepfather occupied a prestigious position as a minister in the Guyanese government. It was all supposed to be a fairy tale life. With the wisdom of retrospection, perhaps my mother was never destined to have a fairy tale life after all.

What started happening was stranger than fiction. Shortly after my arrival in this beautiful setting, my distinguished stepfather; the prominent politician, the respected government minister, started abusing me physically. He would beat me for no reason. He would scream at me for no apparent reason. He treated me worse than a person in prison, and whenever my mother tried to defend me, or come to my rescue, he would beat her mercilessly. Matters degenerated from bad to worse. It had gotten to the point where the abuse was so much that he was now, on daily basis, beating my mother and I. Matters came to a head the night my mother decided she could not take anymore abuse, and would not stay a day longer under his roof.

That fateful night, Mr Minister had beaten my mother rather brutally. He finally stripped her naked, and threw her clothes out through the window, and onto the roof of the house. That part of the roof was over a shed, and so the window was actually overlooking the roof over that shed. At the same time, he had a knife in his hand. My mother somehow managed to dispossess him of the knife, and threw it out through the window. The man grabbed me and put me out through the window to go and bring back the knife. Being only a relatively weightless little girl, I was able to safely crawl on the zinc roofing. However, on reaching the knife, I picked it up and threw it away. Mr Minister was understandably incensed and outraged at my precocious audacity. Livid with anger, he dared me to come back into the house. I did exactly that. He descended on me, and continued to beat me and my mother. He locked us up in the house and went out. As soon as he left, my mother put me out through the same window, and climbing up behind me, we left the house.

Let me take a brief moment to examine the subject of domestic abuse. Why do some men abuse the women in their lives? There is no doubt that the vast majority of physical abuse victims are women. While there is no direct cause of physical abuse, there are factors that are known to increase the risk for physical abuse, both on the side of the perpetrator, and on the side of the victim. It is worth noting that women abused in marriages suffer greater severity of abuse than those in other types of relationships. While no one type of man abuses women, abusive men are known to share certain characteristics. Generally, they tend to have lower levels of education and IQ. They are less clear-thinking. They are more neurotic, anxious, nervous and defensive. They are less less self-confident. They are more excitable, moody, hasty and self-centered. Definitely, they are more authoritarian. These characteristics of men who abuse women alone show that they are more likely to lash out when provoked. Some men even show pride in abusing women. Instead of being ashamed, they seem proud about kicking, biting, or slapping their wives and girlfriends.

The causes of physical abuse may be related to one of the personality characteristics noted above, possibly because of the abuser's desire for unquestioned obedience and their lack of compassion for those they consider weak or inferior. Unfortunately, sexism often rears its ugly head in situations in which men consider women weak and inferior. Thus, when a woman "breaks a rule," the man feels no compunction whatsoever about meting out harsh punishments like physical abuse. However, the causes of physical abuse should not be attributed to sexism alone, and power and control must rank as the prevalent motivations for physical abuse.

Anyway, after we escaped from my stepfather's house, my mother sought sanctuary at the premises of a catholic church. Although I was just a little girl, probably not older than four years, I recall that the priests instructed someone to take us to a member's house, where we remained for about four days, during which time my mother would often go out, presumably trying to source for money for us to go back to Barbice, to my grandmother's house, and also to try to get us food. My stepfather had already taken the baby into his mother's custody. In taking away her baby from her, I can now imagine the trauma she must have felt. He had restricted her from seeing the baby, and had forbidden her from ever venturing near his mother's house. He had even given his mother strict instructions not to let my mother see the baby. She must have been devastated. As a child, while I could see her tears, I definitely could not appreciate the agony she was feeling. My mother was only thirteen years older than I was. That meant, in that year of severe personal trauma in which I was four years old, she would have been only seventeen.

My stepfather somehow found out where we were hiding. That really ought not to come as such a surprise, as he had unlimited resources. He was finance minister in the government of Guyana at the time, and so he had sent out people to search for my mother. They finally tracked us down to the church member's house. Even before then, we had suffered some trauma at that house. Our hosts had a very big dog. One day, the dog bit me. When my mother got back home, she was understandably quite upset, and crying, she asked them how they could have possibly allowed their dog to bite a little child. I will never forget the response of the lady of the house, *"Your daughter was in the dog's way. The dog was not in your daughter's way."*

My mother was merely a young adult. She was still a teenager. Therefore, those times must have been intensely painful for her. In retrospect, it is now easier for me to see how she might have so easily transitioned into an alcoholic. Without doubt, she drowned herself in alcohol to seek the numbness that would disallow her to be in conscious awareness of the tragedy her entire life had become. More significantly, her alcoholic haze all but guaranteed that she needn't feel the need to be responsible. First, you had this young girl who had been torn away from her childhood love, all due to social prejudices and fractures she could not even comprehend. Then, she fell into the hands of a much older man who, after initially assuring her of his love and affection, and impregnating her, had now turned full circle to terrorize her, and use his influence and high office to hound her. I distinctly recall my mother holding me tightly in her arms on the day that dog bit me, and crying her heart out. It was not long after that, on that same day, that Mr Minister found us, and brought us back to his house. We stayed there for about a week, during which time my mother was obviously trying to organize some money for our escape. A week later, we absconded again, and went straight to Berbice, to my grandmother's house.

The experience with Mr Minister must have been the straw that broke the camel's back. Certainly, it was after that series of events that my mother seemed to snap. Clearly, she had become empty of all rational thought and well-adjusted emotions. She had suffered so much abuse, when all she ever desired was to spend time with her children and simply live a fairy tale existence. As all her expectations in that regard were continually dashed, she became emotionally detached from any semblance of reality, and becoming totally distraught, it became impossible for anyone to any longer reach her on any emotional level. In her trauma, she had even lost her beauty at such a tender age, and had fast become a mere shadow of her former self. She had lost her ability to feel with a heart that had been totally broken by society. Now totally lacking in any degree of self-worth, she simply dropped out of sight, and I would not see her again until I was seven years old.

Yet, I never did forgot about her in her absence, even though hardly anyone spoke about her. It was almost as if she had suddenly gone into extinction. It was as if she had never existed. As a child, one tends to become attached to what is available, while one doesn't wonder too much about what is unavailable. Yet, I silently kept a place for my mother in my heart, and I would often fantasize about how, someday, I was going to take care of her, and make her happy. In fact, that was my principal motivation for earning good grades. I wanted to be a successful person who would have a good job and earn good money. I wanted to become somebody important and affluent, so I could take care of my mother, and so that she would not have to go through so much abuse. I no longer wanted I to watch her cry. As matters stood, it seemed as if each time I looked at her, she was sad and crying. The only happy moment I seemed to be able to associate with her was the day she came to take me on that trip away to Georgetown. I believe I have spent my entire life just trying to re-create a similar moment between my mother and I; that moment of mutual bliss in which I would see that happy look in her face. Tragically, no matter how much I tried, I never again saw that look of bliss on my mother's face.

I have often wondered about what makes mothers so special. The reasons are not necessarily that far fetched. Mother is the most beautiful creation of God whose heart is filled with unconditional love. She is always there when needed, provides everything that is desired and cares enough to protect her children from evil. The love of a mother is the purest form of joy that one can ever experience. She never stops caring for you, and always has your best interests at heart. A mother is irreplaceable in our hearts and in our lives. For all practical purposes, your mother is the reason for your existence. All the beautiful things and worldly joys that you are able to witness are because of your mother. She gave birth to you, and assumed the responsibility to love you, care for you, and support you. Your mother is the only person in the entire world who places your needs and happiness before hers. No matter how tired she is, if you were hungry in the middle of the night, she would sacrifice her sleep to ensure that you do not sleep on an empty stomach.

Whenever you are dealing with the tough issues of life, your mother is always there to cheer you up, and to put a broad smile on your face. Her kind words comfort you in the hard times and leave you feeling fresh, confident, and full of life. Your mother is the most prominent figure in your life, and she keeps giving without expecting anything in return. Her selfless love is something you can never ever receive from anyone else in your entire life. She loves you even when you are unhappy with yourself and, almost by definition, it is her affection that makes you a better person. Your mother, in wearing several hats at the same time, and handling all her responsibilities with near-perfection, is the ultimate source of inspiration in your life. She teaches you valuable lessons, supports you at every step, and inspires you to achieve beyond your anticipated potential. She is irreplaceable. The warmth of her love holds a special place in your heart, and continually offers much-needed comfort. People come and go in your life, but it is your mother whom you always hold close to your heart, and she can never be replaced by anyone else on Earth.

Mother is the best therapist on Earth. We all have to deal with a multiplicity of problems on daily basis. Putting your head on your mother's lap after a tiring day can make all the difference. Talking to your mother is like therapy that relaxes your mind and gives you the strength to deal with the world. Mother is not just a word to a child. Mother is the centerpiece of a child's existence. Mother is a child's world. A child's entire life revolves around her, and she is the best thing that ever happened to you. The word "Mother" resonates with the bliss of the unconditional love and care that is the basic need of every child. The bond between children and their mothers appears to be eternal as it starts long before birth. With just one look in a mother's eye towards her child, and we arrive at the real meaning of unconditional love. To adequately express a mother's love in words is a Herculean task. For a mother, a child always remains her baby, even if she turns 60, or becomes the nation's president.

For a child, the process of learning starts right from birth, or even before it. During pregnancy, mothers are encouraged to read good books aloud, and listen to soothing music. They do this because, although still a fetus, the baby is assumed to be already developing a connection with the world through its mother. Later, the baby is acquainted with the world, first by her mother, and later by others. Whatever the language, caste or custom, every baby learns to call her mother first. "Mama" is the first word that comes out from a baby's mouth. A mother teaches her child everything that she knows, right from talking and walking, and on to living a fulfilling life. She is also the one who disciplines and educates a child for a better life. Right from the time of awakening to bedtime, a mother is at duty teaching her child. In fact, a mother is necessarily constrained to go through the process of learning all over again, just to help her child receive premium knowledge from her.

Mothers give hope. If it weren't for mothers, this world would be a hopeless place. Life is a mixed grill of experiences, some of which can be downright unpleasant. A child faces all these right from the cradle, but it is her mother who, with her love, care and comfort, assures that she safely traverses this treacherous terrain. Through her eyes and confidence, a child will always see light at the other end of the tunnel. Whether facing examination, competitions or the hardships of life, children always seek guidance and support from their mothers first. That is hardly surprising. For a mother, her child is an open book. She knows her child like no other person. Whatever the child feels, the mother knows it, and nothing remains hidden from her. She is the best judge of her child's personality, and she makes sure that the child is treated and disciplined accordingly. Knowing her child's interests and needs, she accommodates new changes for the betterment and overall development of her child.

Mothers are the foundations and pillars of our lives. We all need that person on whom we can fall back on in times of crisis, especially emotional ones. What can possibly be better than the arms of a mother, where all the problems, insecurities and negative feelings find a willing dumping ground? A child will always need the support of a mother, no matter the phase of life; schooling, marriage, or having a baby. She is the one who acts like a strong pillar on which a child can always depend. My conclusion is that we can never fully pay back for whatever a mother has done, and continues to do for us. All we can do is reciprocate the same love and affection. Though a mother will never ask anything in return for her love, care and protection, we can always reciprocate her love with those little gestures that make her feel special. Despite the tragedy of our joint lives, I will always cherish those special moments I shared with my mother.

As I earlier mentioned, although I seem to have spent my entire life just trying to re-create that special moment between my mother and I when she came to take me with her to Georgetown, that moment of mutual bliss continued to elude me, and no matter how much I tried, I never again saw that look of bliss on her face. Rather, I have been left with memories of the episodes of abuse that I suffered on the occasions when I had to go and live with her. Those experiences were as terrifying as they were painful. By now, Ena, my mother, had become a confirmed alcoholic who did not care about herself, talk less of caring about me. She had become practically numb to any semblance of a conventional existence, and lived merely to exist. Totally heartbroken and confused, she wallowed distractedly in a state of deep depression, and drifted from one day to the next in an alcoholic haze. Her very existence centered around a cycle of sleeping and drinking. She would drink until she passed out. When she awakened from her alcohol-induced stupor, she would embark on the same process all over again. She was never in short supply of alcohol. It was always available. That was not surprising. She was a very beautiful woman, and men, quickly recognizing her bottomless crave for alcohol, used her addiction to easily take advantage of her. She was never in critical supply of the men willing to offer her alcohol. They encouraged her to drink, and bought her the drinks. They took her out to drink, just so that she could become sufficiently inebriated for them to have their way with her.

When I lived with her, we shared a little eight-by-ten room that we called home. It had only one bed, one table, two chairs and a kerosene lamp. It was customary for my mother to sleep on the bed with whichever bedfellow visited her for the night. I slept on the ground, right next to the bed, a perfectly unwilling witness to the sexual exploitation and degradation of my own mother. As might be expected, the men also sought to have their way with me. When they failed in their bid to have sex with me, they encouraged my mother to abuse me. Almost on daily basis, I received a beating from a mother who, in totally lacking in any volition of her own, simply did whatever she was told. One day, while I was in the midst of preparations for an examination, I asked my mother for the reason why I was getting such a terrible beating. I recall that I was literally screaming at her, demanding to know why I was getting such a severe beating from her. My mother's response was as comical as it was nonsensical. She accused me of always reading, and poking my nose into her affairs. She further accused me of reading all her important papers. She said she was tired of my reading. At the end of that day's beating, I threw all my schoolbooks into what we called a barrel, and set them on fire, vowing never to ever again open another book, since my quest for an education was obviously responsible for the

86

horrendous abuse I was subjected to. In order words, if I had to stop reading to stop the abuse, so be it. Yet, my desire for excellence soon led me right back to my quest for an education. That seemed to be the only thing I could hold on to. As matters stood, I felt my life was valueless. I felt like a garbage can. I seemed to possess no value to anyone around me. I felt treated, not as someone existing as a person, but more like 'something' fit only for convenient abuse. To compensate for these feelings of unworthiness, not only was my quest for an education stronger than ever, but I also wished to attain excellence and perfection. That, in all essence, appeared to be the only way I could become a person of value.

On another occasion, my mother came home in the wee hours of the morning, drunk and screaming hysterically. She was crying and screaming at the same time. There was no way to tell exactly what time of the morning it was. The only way to estimate the time was a whistle that blew at 5am, 6am and 7am at the nearby bauxite plant to alert workers on time milestones with regards to their work. Also, school children knew that when the third whistle blew, it was time to set out for school. Sometime before the first whistle blew at 5am, my mother came home screaming hysterically. At some point, she took some pills with a glass of water. I did not realize that my mother had taken sleeping pills in her drunken state. I merely thought she was in a drunken stupor as usual. As fate would have it, I read the label on the bottle at the side of the bed. It was a bottle of sleeping pills. I tried to wake my mother up, but all she did was mutter the ominous words, "I'm dying…." I was totally confused and absolutely terrified. I ran out in search of help. Naturally, help was nowhere close by, so I ran a couple of miles to the nearest hospital, hoping to get the attention of the nurses and doctors who might come home with me with an ambulance to help my mother.

I ran along a train track that served as guide to get to the hospital. Absolutely petrified, I kept on running, thinking all the while that if I didn't run fast enough, and didn't get to the hospital fast enough, my mother would die. I also recoiled from the horror of being blamed for her death because I didn't get help to her soon enough. It was a very terrifying experience for a child. Somehow, I managed to get to the hospital, and an ambulance took me back to the house. My mother was taken to the hospital, where her stomach was pumped of everything. Although, after this terrifying incident, life assumed a semblance of normalcy, I had been transformed into a nervous wreck, as I became paranoiacally vigilant and concerned about my mother's state of mind, convinced that she might once again try to kill herself. My ever present dread was that such a terrible thing might happen in my absence. Therefore, in addition to my feelings of neglect and abuse, I developed a real and foreboding fear of the prospect of helplessly allowing my mother to die due to my own carelessness, or worse, being labeled my own mother's killer. Suffice it to say that it was a terrible state of mind for a child to be in.

It was the combination of these terrifying, frightening and nerve-wracking experiences that propelled me inexorably into a nervous breakdown at a period that coincided with one of my father's vacation visits to Guyana. He had requested that I come back and live in his house. Being, as usual, an obedient and respectful child, I went back to my father's house, and his club, the Boatsman Club, and assumed duties as cook and cleaner. As usual, I went back to doing all of the household chores. One day, however, when everything appeared to have entered a state of calm, and life seemed to be proceeding with a tranquil routine, all hell broke loose. I had just finished cooking for everyone in the house, and I sat down quietly after doing all my work. Suddenly, I seemed to explode. I started screaming, shouting and stomping my feet on the ground. I was totally out of control in an episode that required twelve grown men to contain me, and tie me up. I was instantly taken to an obeah man, since the consensus was that I was possessed by demons. In retrospect, it is obvious that I was actually suffering a severe nervous breakdown occasioned by the accumulated effects of emotional, physical and mental abuse. My little system was on overdrive, and could take no more trauma. Naturally, and as was the usual practice, I was tied up and dragged to the obeah man who, as would be expected, proclaimed that I was possessed by demons, and of course, I was given some horrible concoction to drink, while I had a mixture of strange fluids poured all over me in the form a bath that would exorcise me of the demons. I slept for twenty four hours. Since I woke up calm and quiet, it was assumed that the demons had left me.

8

The Dotted Line

On the sixth day of October of the year 1975, at the tender age of fifteen, I gave birth to my first child. He was given the names Paul Anthony Halley, aka Cecil Levine. History, in the most uncanny of manners, was unwittingly repeating itself. My own mother had given birth to me at an even younger age. Ena Subryan was only twelve years of age when she gave birth to me. By any known empirical standard, it was a classic case of a baby mothering a baby. Indeed, I was nothing more than a child of a child.

Perhaps the greatest tragedy in this precocious experience of early motherhood was my total and unmitigated ignorance of *'the facts of life'* that inexorably led to it in the first place. We all know the story of *"the birds and the bees,"* which is an age-old metaphor for explaining the physiologic dynamics of reproduction to younger children. The metaphor, of course, relies on the imagery of pollination by bees, and the subsequent hatching of eggs, as a rather convenient substitute for the more seemingly embarrassing technical, graphic description and lurid explanation of sexual intercourse.

90

For the reader who is still be in the dark about this convenient alternative to graphic sex education, according to tradition, *"the birds and the bees"* is a metaphorical story sometimes related to children in an attempt to explain the mechanics and results of sexual intercourse by referring to easily observable natural events. As it happens, bees carry and deposit pollen into flowers, in much the same visible and easy-to-explain parallel manner that a man fertilizes a woman's eggs with spermatozoa. By the same token, the laying of eggs by female birds is a similarly visible and easily comprehensible parallel to female ovulation. All these are ingenious ways of deflecting the inevitable question that every parent dreads, *"Where do babies come from?"*

Tragically, I was not accorded even the innocent privilege of asking that seemingly embarrassing question of a mother with whom I was largely at odds most of the time, or a father who was totally absent from my life at that tender age. I was neither familiar with the term *menstrual cycle,* nor had I the faintest inkling of any concept of the physical sex act at the time of that first experience that instantly resulted in pregnancy. Naturally, whatever significance and function that could be ascribed to a concept of sex that I was entirely unfamiliar with also meant little or no sense to me. I was also totally in the dark about the biological functions of a body that was in the same instant a total stranger to me as I grew up. In accurate summary, I gave birth to my first child at the age of fifteen years in the absence of any semblance of understanding of the dynamics of sex, the function of sex, the importance of sex, the negative impacts of early teenage pregnancy, the details of the process of gestation itself, and ultimately, the consequences of intimate interaction between a man and a woman.

My baby was born at New Amsterdam Hospital, in Berbice, Guyana. For me, it was a near-magical experience holding that little infant in my arms for the first time. Yet, the entire traumatic experience leading up to childbirth was anything but magic. I was rushed to the hospital in excruciating pain at barely seven months of gestation. At least, I had been fed the correct information that the normal duration of a pregnancy was supposed to be nine months. So, what had happening to me? Naturally, I was not to know that the combination of severe malnourishment and living each stressful day, one agonizingly stressful day at a time, was not the most propitious circumstances under which an underage woman could possibly successfully carry a pregnancy to full term. Throughout the duration of my pregnancy, I was living with Cecil Levine, a registered nurse working at the Berbice Asylum, otherwise known as the Berbice Madhouse. Levine was basically my caretaker, although in real and practical terms, I saw him more as the protector who delivered me from the extreme trauma I went through in the hands of my mother and stepfather, the man my mother was living with at that time. The entire house itself had four apartments, and my mother lived in one of the apartments, while Levine lived in another. I had ended up at Levine's apartment after he had rescued me from Canje Bridge, saving me from jumping off the bridge to commit suicide in the wake of the trauma my mother had subjected me to, and in which she had deliberately boiled some water, and thrown it at me in self-righteous anger because I had blatantly refused to get married to Cliff Halley, the soldier whose child I was carrying. Cliff Halley had made regular trips to my mother at Canje, Berbice, in those hectic months in which my mother and I lived together. He always came bearing gifts and money, all in an effort to induce my mother to encourage me to marry him. Yet, I remained adamant in my refusal to marry the man.

I did not want to be married to Cliff Halley for the simple reason that the mere thought of having sex with him on a regular basis was as scary to me as it was altogether unfathomable. Cliff Halley was the first man I would sleep with. It was not a pleasant introduction to sexual intimacy. I was decidedly not in love with the man. Most certainly, there wasn't the faintest whiff of romance in our tumultuous relationship. I merely used the only currency available to me to pay a debt. That currency was the combination of my immature body, and an ill-understood sexuality. I was just a child who allowed a man to have sex with her in abject ignorance of what the act itself actually entailed, and its inevitable consequence. Cliff Halley was paying my bills when I was staying with the woman my mother had abandoned me with, deceitfully giving the impression that the woman was my grandmother, resulting in yet another situation in which I was left with an entire stranger whose only intention was to abuse me. I cleaned the house, shopped for groceries, cooked the food, did the laundry, and did just about anything else that required the exertion of human labor. It was during this time that Cliff Halley offered to pay my lady guardian money for my upkeep and maintenance. This state of affairs subsisted for quite some time. Several months later, Cliff Halley commenced the initial subterranean efforts to sleep with me. At first, I did not know what to make of overtures that I was not only totally unfamiliar with, but whose significance was lost on me. Although the initial pressure was quite subliminal, all I knew was that Mr Halley, my exceedingly generous benefactor, wanted something from me. I knew no one else. The man was paying my bills, a gesture that somewhat eased the ordeal of the abuse I was subjected to. So, instead of the regular beatings I received at the hands of my lady guardian, all I now had to endure was verbal abuse. With this relief came the realization that I was obligated in some way or the other to Cliff Halley.

There was absolutely no doubt about the fact that he had effected an unexpected improvement in the quality of my life. Most certainly, I was unaware of anyone else I could even remotely consider family or friend at that time. My mother had not bothered to return since she left, and there was no information about her whereabouts. I also had no knowledge about any existing relative anywhere. I was all alone with Mr Halley. He was my only ally. Eventually, I had to pay my debt to him, and Mr Halley had sex with me. Incredibly, I did not even recognize the act itself as sex. All I knew was that Mr Halley wanted it and, on my own part, I merely saw my acquiescence to his demand as some kind of sacrifice in which, by allowing him access to my body; to forcefully invade my body, I was paying back a huge debt that I owed the man. It was, not unnaturally, a painful initiation to an act that was not in my immediate best interest. The experience itself, in addition to its consequence, basically added up to why I did not want to marry Mr Halley. Nothing else mattered more than avoiding such a marriage. I neither considered my own financial and social security, nor did I consider that of my unborn child. In any case, I was entirely unaware that there was any potential security in a marriage, as there were no role models to look up to in that regard, neither was there anyone around to educate me about the process of growing up, and the responsibilities incident to adulthood. All I had ever experienced in my life was abuse and manipulation from the adults that were around me.

I was intentional with the choice of title for my biography, *Child of A Child*. Indeed, I was a child plunged prematurely and precociously into the world of adults. The Good Book says, *"When I was a child, I talked like a child, I thought like a child, I reasoned like a child............"* That means, if as a child, one thinks and acts like a child, it can only beat the imagination to expect a child to function as an adult in an adult world in which one is prematurely treated as an adult. How can a girl-child be expected to understand the implications of having sexual relations with a grown man? How can a girl-child be expected to grasp the responsibilities inherent in having sexual relations with a grown man? In many respects, I consider myself uncommonly fortunate to have somehow managed to develop into fully-functioning adulthood, devoid of the possible devastating consequences of such a psychologically traumatic childhood. Not many people are that fortunate. That, in fact, is one of the principal reasons why society is afflicted with an entire generation of psychologically incapacitated adults who seemingly remain children throughout a totally dysfunctional lifetime. These days, I am at a vantage position to ask questions, such as, *"How can children be protected from the sexually exploitative actions of predators?" "How can children be better educated, from an early age, about the facts of life, and the more sordid aspects of those facts?"*

Children are giving birth to children. That is a stark fact in today's world. On the surface, this statement is seemingly about the practice of child marriage. In some African cultures, people see a girl who begins menstruating as ready to marry. Yet, girls' minds and bodies are not yet ready to become mothers. There is a significant social effect as well. Girls who are only biologically

94

able to have children are really not yet ready for the emotional burden of parenthood, nor do they have a job or business that can support them both. Almost by definition, they haven't yet finished schooling, and most of the time, a girl who becomes a mother will not finish school at all. Her personal development will come to an abrupt end. Her dreams and goals for her future will end, and the future of her child is compromised by her own lower status in society.

By the year 2000, the United Nations estimated that developing countries had about one billion adolescents who were physically old enough to reproduce themselves, but still far too young to be responsible, healthy parents of healthy children. The United Nations has encouraged governments to become more involved in the issues surrounding adolescent pregnancy, even suggesting that both custom and the laws must change to reflect the needs of young people. The consequences of early childbearing are felt by society as well as the families directly affected. Childbirth amongst very young women, both married and unmarried is growing. Each year approximately 13 million children are born to young mothers. The percentage of live births to mothers under the age of 20 ranges from 20% in some African and Caribbean countries; 10-15% in many Latin American countries, 5-10% in Asia, and 1% in Japan. Increased out-of-wedlock adolescent pregnancy is due to many factors, and include earlier sexual maturity, increased opportunity for opposite sex interaction in schools, and rapid urbanization which weakens traditional family structures and social and cultural controls.

Early childbirth is especially dangerous for adolescents and their infants. Compared to women between the ages of 20-35, pregnant women under 20 are at a greater risk for death and disease, including bleeding during pregnancy, toxemia, hemorrhage, prolonged and difficult labor, severe anemia, and disability. Life-long social and economic disadvantages may be a consequence of teenage birth. Educational and career opportunities may be limited, as may be opportunities for marriage. Teenage mothers tend to have larger completed family sizes, shorter birth intervals resulting in both poorer health status for the family, and a more severe level of poverty. The children also suffer since teenage mothers tend to have a higher incidence of low birth weight infants which is associated with birth injuries, serious childhood illness, and mental and physical disabilities. Adolescent access to family planning information and services is limited. Government programs in developing countries have focused on older women to limit family size. In addition, national laws and local customs often prohibit minors from consenting to medical services. Both the number and proportions of abortions performed for young women have been increasing. Abortions are more physically traumatic for young women who tend to request services later in pregnancy.

The girl-child must be protected. They must be properly cared for. They must be appropriately guided into adulthood. Certain vital and unavoidable steps are necessary on the journey from the cradle to the grave, which essentially translates to 'from birth to adulthood.' The steps of human growth are as inexorable as they are inevitable; baby, toddler, young child, teenager, young adult, adult, middle age and old age. Each of these stages is a step in the growth process, and each step has its own expectations in terms of knowledge and wisdom. The reason for this gradual, step-by-step development is simple. In order to gain a full experience of life in all its natural and healthy ramifications, we must encounter and pass through these steps of life, in the process gaining all the education that each step has on offer, before graduating to the next step. Along the journey, we are both educated and nurtured, and we glean information that is appropriate for each stage of our development. The expectations of children are vastly different from the expectations of adults. This is because education, experience and knowledge-gathering processes are also vastly different at the different stages of development. As a child grows, the brain grows. As the brain is exposed to more and more knowledge, education is essentially being received, such that the child becomes equipped to deal with the exigencies of life, and to handle life and situations in its various presentations. When a blind man is led into a fire pit, it is only when the fire sears him, and starts to burn his clothes and his skin that he realizes the danger he is in. Children are perfectly innocent human beings. They are, not unnaturally, quite excited about living and life, and of course, without the vital protection of the education and nurturing of parents and guardians, they are left vulnerable to just about any sort of danger that adult society can present. If we do not establish proper processes to protect children in an adult world, we will continue to have children that are subjected to vicious cycles of malfunction and dysfunction, and the more fractured society will continue to be.

A child that gives birth to another child is a broken piece of equipment, no more, no less. To attach a broken piece of equipment to another structure is simply and merely to wittingly invite an avoidable accident. Without doubt as, with the hindsight of experience, I now believe and preach, humanity needs strong structures to create a stronger world than we have now. I believe we cannot have the stability and strength that we deserve when we continually have two broken pieces attached together. The weak connection represented by these two broken pieces can only provide for a weaker structure and a weaker society. It is our obligation to establish protective programs and protective environments for our children. Education is key. Families must have support in the home, so that they can, in turn, support their children in those homes, so that these children can be allowed to have a life that will nurture them into fully-functioning adulthood by providing them with the tools that are needed to arrive at the appropriate decisions. More often than not, children are not really given a chance to have any input about decisions that impact them. Decisions are made about them, and for them, that place them in vulnerable situations in which they are invariably exposed to danger, yet they remain as absolutely clueless as the blind man being led into a fire pit, of the danger that adult society can very starkly pose to such innocence.

My son is now a fully grown adult, and he still hasn't a clue about the harrowing process I went through at his birth. For instance, the name on his birth certificate is not the name that I actually chose for him. That alone also underscores the fact that, as a juvenile mother, you are neither familiar with the structure and dynamics of giving birth, nor are you conversant with the essence of naming a child, having a birth certificate or even the process involved in the registration of a birth. I never provided information for the registration of my child at the hospital. I was very ill, and actually went into a coma when the child was born prematurely, as I developed a complication known as *septicemia*, a severe infection of the blood circulatory system. As a matter of fact, because of this, my baby left the hospital before I did. The gentleman named Mr Levine, who was a nurse at that time, signed the birth certificate. I was not even aware that my baby required a certificate of birth. I was appallingly uneducated about a lot of things, as I did not complete my schooling at that time, having been robbed of the opportunity to become properly educated, and thrown into the streets to barely survive.

Naturally, I was also totally ignorant of my responsibilities as as a mother, one of which was to see to the proper registration of my baby's name. My own mother was only twelve years old when she had me, and what she went through can only be imagined. As it happened, when I was born, the name on my birth certificate read Monica Subryan, yet it was not until I commenced my elementary school education that I became aware that my name was Monica; the name given the school authorities, as hitherto I had all the while been known by the nickname 'Donna,' which was the name by which I was known throughout my teenage years. I had never seen my birth certificate. If I was not aware that any such document even remotely existed in my own name, nor even ever seen it before, how could I have possibly known how secure my own son's birth certificate?

This is a reflection of the gross inadequacies that can easily attend a fractured and dysfunctional foundation to life, and these are the sort of dislocations that can easily compromise one's opportunities in early life. In such traumatic circumstances, only a few will survive and rise up, while the rest will most certainly suffer and wither away in abusive and dysfunctional situations. I managed to survive the *dotted line* of my life only because my pain gave me added impetus to fervently desire and seek something different for my own child. It was a decision to protect this child from having to go through my type of traumatic journey. I firmly resolved that my child was never going to experience what I had experienced. I would fight, and find a way to protect the child; to educate the child for a much better future, and a much better life. I would love the child, all the way from being a child to becoming an adult, and see him through all the natural processes that are incident to his birthright; a birthright that is given to every human being, to grow steadily, and in a normal progression, from being a baby to being a child, to being a young adult, to being an adult, and finally, to being an old person in a healthy and humane social structure. This is a process that is a right and not a privilege.

For me, this is now a compelling global issue that has relevance in every cultural environment, and in every social setting in which children are giving birth to children. For me, this has become a compelling personal crusade in which I believe that a primary interest of governments all over the globe must be to offer greater protection for their citizens, especially in the vulnerable age groups, and to lay more emphasis on strategies for survival within such age groups. I believe that although I survived, and my children survived, there are countless many all over the world that are not fortunate enough to cross that *dotted line* of survival. I remain eternally grateful for the privilege to be alive to tell the story of the dotted line of my life, and that is why I have committed to a life in which I will work tirelessly towards massive development in the social structures of society all over the globe, such that the world can move farther and farther away from the phenomenon of children having children without guidance, education, nurturing and protection.

9

Honing My Intellect

"Education is the passport to the future, for tomorrow belongs to those who prepare for it today." - Malcolm X

If there is any one particular trait that stands out about me, it is my fervent inclination towards education. I have always taken to reading like fish takes to water. Reading has always been such a part of me that, even when I was homeless, and living on the streets, I found myself, not only reading to take the harsh bite out of my unfortunate circumstances, but also reading for the pleasure and benefit of others. Ironically, in an inverse paradox of sorts, it was actually my desire to be educated that was seemingly responsible for the greater majority of my woes. For some inexplicable reason, those that ought to be happy to see me become a better version of myself were also the ones bent on thwarting my every effort in that regard.

I was always curious about improvement of any sort, and in anything. I was always fascinated with excellence. I was the neatest little child you could ever encounter. My school uniform, even though I possessed only one set, was always spotless and immaculate. Perhaps the only reason I can attribute to my penchant for excellence and elegance in all I did was that I somehow saw myself in a special light that bordered on combined royalty and regality. I recall that I was often sarcastically referred to as *'little white girl.'* I indulged an acute self-consciousness. As a child, I was shy and introspective. I was very quiet, and only spoke when spoken to. Yet, I had a keen sense of observation, as I noticed everything and everyone around me. I was always busy finding ways to fix things that didn't seem right, or place items in their proper place. If I as much as found a house dirty, I could never rest until I restored it to sparkling cleanliness.

I was also inclined to rectitude in conduct, and was a stickler for what was proper. I would often speak up if I noticed something improper going on around me, even though it might be considered not my place to do so, which often got me into trouble, and earning me a punishment. I had realized from a very early age that I was a very intelligent child, despite the fact that I was not given the privilege of attending private school like my sisters and my cousin. Despite this lack of elitist education, I remained a very curious child. Certainly, I recall that adults around me constantly referred to me as a smart kid. Perhaps no one saw the great potential in me more than my father's mother. She recognized the qualities of success in me, and it was for this reason that she was determined to suppress me, and to make sure that the promise in me never saw the light of day. In other words, the promise of great future potential in me was the reason for the severe punishment I suffered at the hands of my paternal grandmother, because of which I obligatorily became a bit more sensitive to my own child, and indeed, to other children and other mothers.

In my quest to be more intelligent, and more intellectual, I always stood out amongst my sisters and my cousin, and everyone else around me. I was averagely more interested in learning, as I would read the newspapers and any books that were around me. Also, I tried my best to be a good listener at conversations, often interjecting to offer advice to others about what I thought they could do to improve themselves. To complement this cerebral disposition, I devoted scrupulous attention to my hair, while I was also immaculately well-appointed in my dressing. I ensured that I always looked like a million dollars. Not unnaturally, because I was so organized into a neat, little package, and so attentive to the positive things around me, I tended to magnetize people to me. Others were understandably fascinated with me, and would often make favorable comments about me. This led me to the discovery of a fundamental aspect of human nature.

People like nice things. People love beauty. People love and respect excellence in others. People tend to gravitate towards the best version of all that is around them. Armed with this wisdom, I decided that I was going to be the very best that I could possibly be, and so at that tender age of 15, as a young single mother, I made a commitment to myself that I was going to leave my mark on this world. The immediate and significant consequence of that decision was that I found myself closer to God. I seemed to have arrived at the realization that He was my friend. He was my mentor. He was my teacher. He was my savior. He was the only person that would not betray me. I needed someone who would listen to me without judgement. I needed someone who would be my friend, and be unconditionally there for me, in quite the same way I was there for my child.

As matters stood, I could not trust, or depend on any of the adults in my life. They were all so superficial and unreal. My relationship with my father was an interesting case study. My father was reintroduced into my life by my mother who, in acting like a dog in search of a bone, was always excited at the prospect of anything and everything that offered itself as an opportunity for her to arrest the attention of this man who was clearly and unrepentantly the consuming love of her life. As soon as he reappeared in Guyana on one of his holiday trips, and my mother found out about his arrival, she wasted no time in trying to convince me to allow my father back into my life. By this time, I had taken several trips to hell and back on account of his mother, Salome. Quite understandably, I was also in a state of severe disenchantment, if not simmering anger, with him for exposing me to such mistreatment and refusing to intervene to save me from his mother's malevolence. Since he appeared content not to acknowledge my suffering at the hands of his mother, I declined my mother's request to go back into his life. My mother, a woman totally addled with unremitting love, would simply not give up. She finally succeed in pressurizing me into taking my infant son to see his grandfather.

Sometime during that visit, or thereabouts, my father claimed that he had no knowledge whatsoever of the extent of the torture and torment his mother had subjected me to. He promised that he was going to make it up to me. To that effect, he said he would provide a home for me and my baby, and he would ensure that I would be able to complete my schooling and get my diploma. That was, naturally, music to my ears as I was determined to ensure that my son would not have to endure the sort of life I had endured, and the only way I could be assured of that was to acquire an education, and obtain a college degree. I had to finish school so that I could provide adequately for this child. I needed a better paying job. My conviction was total and uncompromising. I would do anything to improve myself by getting a good education, so that I could provide a better life than I had led, at least up till now, for this child. It was this overpowering and overwhelming desire to hone my intellect that finally brought me back to the famous boatman's club, my father's residence and bar restaurant, and back into the life of Grandmother Salome, Queen of my father's castle.

Matters instantly glided back into what I had previously experienced. If Grandmother Salome had previously been a very difficult and malicious woman, she had now become a monster. To express it more dramatically, she transformed from *grandmother* to *grandmonster*. My reappearance in her life only seemed to reignite the resentment, anger, and hatred she harbored towards me. The circumstances were now different. I was no longer alone. I was back in the house with a baby, and my father was also in the house, so her actions towards me had to be tailored to fit in with prevailing situation. As it were, my father was blissfully unaware of the magnitude of hatred and hostility his mother entertained towards me, his own daughter, and her own granddaughter. Yet, even the joint presence of herself, me and my father was still not sufficient to curtail her malevolent excesses. As soon as I arrived back at the boatman's club, she started to harass me. She visited the vilest of curses upon me at every turn, and at everybody opportunity, especially as soon as my father's back was turned. As long as my father was not within earshot, Grandmother Salome unleashed verbal mayhem on me.

Although I now didn't have to do all the slave work I previously did, I still had to wash the dishes, do the laundry, and scrub the floors, since, in any case, I was trained to do this. That aspect of the work also came naturally to me, being someone who simply loathed a filthy environment. I loved to see things looking nice, neat and tidy. Additionally. I had never been a lazy person. My father, for instance, never had an issue with me. He was a practicing dentist. Almost invariably, anytime he was in Guyana on a visit, his patients would book appointments to consult with him. Because I loved to learn, I was always willing to offer him assistance in whatever I could competently handle. I would often help him in making impressions for his dentures, and in sundry other little things in his dental practice. I clearly recall a day on which I was helping my father in his clinic. He had a patient with him. My grandmother appeared to have totally lost control of herself, as she simply let loose a tirade of curses on me. My father had a cup of water in his hand. Suddenly, unable to further keep his feelings in check, he threw the cup of water my grandmother, and screamed at her saying, *"If I have to kill you to get you to stop tormenting this child, then I will gladly do so! Stop it! Leave her alone!"*

Everyone, including my grandmother, froze in their tracks. Grandmother Salome virtually turned into an ice queen. Her look of total disbelief was a sight to behold. Between the onlookers and my grandmother, I don't know who was more shocked at my father's display of anger at his mother. My father was the youngest child of his mother, and he was the apple of her eye, just as much as he doted upon her. He loved his mother to uncommon distraction. He adored her unconditionally. He gave her anything and everything to install her in near-obscene comfort. Anything and everything she ever wanted or needed was at her beck and call. He had never been known to raise his voice at her, and had never be seen to argue with her. He never ever opposed her on any issue. I relate this extreme devotion and fealty of my father to his mother to fully underscore the significance of what transpired that day in his dental office. Quite frankly, to throw the cup of water at her was considered near unimaginable enough. For him to now threaten to kill his mother, even if he had to, if that was what it would take to get her to stop tormenting his child, was totally out of this world.

Yet, even her son's uncharacteristic outburst and anger did nothing to stop this woman from tormenting me. In all truth, there were no valid reasons for my grandmother to make my life hell on Earth. Admittedly, I was a neat little child. Admittedly, I was a dutiful and helpful little child. Admittedly, I read everything that I found lying around, and because I genuinely sought to improve myself and others, I even read to her and for her. Instead of appreciating that I was of help to her on all conceivable fronts, she accused me of being 'nosy,' and that I wanted to know all about her business, so that I could later turn against her and hurt her. Each time she found me reading information in and around the house, she accused me of trying to find out all about her business, so that I could hurt her. Yet, I was a mere child. What could a mere child possibly do to hurt a business she knew practically nothing about? My grandmother continued to have a field day tormenting me until my father finally came to my rescue.

My father kept his word. Yes, my father, against whom I had harbored deep seated ill feelings for seemingly turning a blind eye to his mother's ill treatment of me, actually kept his word to me about charting out out a new course for my life, and for my infant son and I, and my life took on a brighter look. A few months after arriving at the boatman's club, in which I had to endure another round of excruciating and bitter maltreatment from my grandmother, my father, son and myself left our country, Guyana, for Canada. Shortly after our arrival in Canada, I enrolled myself in school to continue my education. But as my life of unfortunate events would once again have it, if I even remotely thought I had arrived at my happy ending, I was making a grave mistake. Apparently, my father had helped a few family members to migrate to Canada. What I still cannot conclusively say is if these family members were in some form of communication or the other with my grandmother, or whether the series of unfortunate events that rapidly unfolded was based on my grandmother's instruction, but what I can write on these pages is that some people reported me to Canadian immigration authorities. Naturally. I was on a visitor's visa. The immigration officers came looking for me. They picked me up, and I was placed under a detention order. Yet, as a combination of fate and divine providence would have it, possibly due to a close relationship I now enjoyed with God, the immigration officer that picked me up would yet turn out an advisor of sorts. He counseled me exhaustively on how to firmly secure my stay in Canada. While I only had to endure an overnight stay at that detention center, that brief stay was all I needed to gain familiarity with all the ammunition I needed to get out of there, and to permanently establish myself in Canadian society without the threat of deportation.

Whilst I was in detention, I was not only offered free advice by the immigration officers on how to legalize my immigrant status, but was also educated on how to formally extend my stay until I could legalize my status. In the event, my brief spat with the immigration actually turned out a blessing in disguise. In fact, it was almost as if they were sent to me, not necessarily to punish me or deport me for violating visa regulations, but to set me firmly on the path to the regularization of my immigration status. In effect, therefore, whoever reported me to the immigration authorities, whether in cahoots with my grandmother or not, was actually divinely sent to me as a big favor and unquantifiable blessing. In my life journey, I have learnt that, sometimes, when people constitute themselves into your traducers, what they don't know is that they are unwittingly working in your favor. People seem to forget that there is a God out there looking out for His own. Also, in my love walk with God, I have learnt to be grateful in all things. Indeed, I am grateful to those people for going to the Canadian authorities to spill the beans about my immigration status. They merely did me an immense favor by making my path to status regulation simpler and clearer.

As soon as I came out of detention, I continued my education. Part of the advice I was given was that being a student would help my case in the long run. That was how my young son and I started to adjust to a different way of life in this strange, and very cold land. I felt so loved, and was immensely grateful that I was given another chance at life in Canada. Shortly after my arrival in Canada, I found some members of my extended family who had previously relocated to Canada. I also reunited with my friend, Roxanne. Roxanne and her family had earlier migrated to Canada. In reuniting with them, I was also able to renew my friendship with her older sister, Patsy, who started to mentor me since she was a school teacher, and now worked at a bank in Canada. I found myself spending a lot of time with her, and since she was an educator, being in her company only served to push me a little harder in my attempt to hone and honor my intellect. I developed such a strong passion for learning that I enrolled in many classes outside of my own basic curriculum. I enrolled in classes that taught arts and crafts, including candle making and basket making. I literally enrolled myself in anything and everything that I could enroll myself into. To say that I was riding on a euphoric intellectual high would be putting my combined elation and exhilaration rather too mildly. I was exceedingly happy with my new way of life. Whenever I found myself in a new learning program, my whole world seemed to explode in a kaleidoscope of beautiful colors, and everything not only appeared bright and shiny, but everything was also good and wonderful. Learning actually became my drug of choice during this period of my life. More significantly, it led me to meeting my husband, Israel Sanchez.

Israel Sanchez was serving in the army. He totally defined the word 'wonderful.' To declare that the man changed my life would be putting his remarkable influence on me rather mildly. If, before I met him, I had always considered myself royalty of sorts, Israel Sanchez introduced me to an entirely new definition of the word 'royalty.' He made me realize that

I was, indeed, a queen. His treatment of me transcended the ordinary to occupy a pedestal that I never imagined was even remotely possible in any relationship I could possibly have with a man. His brand of love was so new to me that I had to constantly pinch myself to confirm that I was experiencing it in real life, and not just dreaming it. He was kind to me. He was patient with me. He respected me. He adored me. He nurtured me. He treated me as an extremely special person. Before I met him, I was totally unaware of what it meant to be in a relationship with someone. I was blissfully ignorant of what the mutual responsibilities of participants in a relationship were. My husband met all those responsibilities with more than creditable aplomb, and more.

I would eventually leave Canada, and migrate to the United States with my children and my husband, as his family lived in America. My husband provided a very nice home for me. He was loving, attentive, caring and totally devoted, and one could not ask for more. He worked hard to provide for us as a military personnel. Yet, despite all these good tidings, my traumatic past was about to take its unfortunate toll on the idyllic setting in which I found myself. In retrospect, I can now see that when you take a fractured person, one such as myself, and you place this fractured person beside someone who is wholesome and beautiful, you are bound to precipitate a conflict, or an incongruence, as it were.

Even though my husband tried his best to be a loving, caring and devoted partner, I was obviously such *'damaged goods'* that I could not even remotely appreciate the beauty of his personality, and the enormous potential for good that he represented in my life. Clearly, I was even blind to the extent of his commitment to me. I was so broken from my past trauma that it was difficult to recognize true love and affection when it was freely and unconditionally offered. One day, a mild argument ensued between us and, of course, the broken woman in me blew it totally out of proportion. I somehow managed to convert a mere disagreement into a *tempest in a teacup*. A *storm in a teacup* is a British idiom which refers to an event of minute dimension that has been blown out of proportion. It's American equivalent is 'a *tempest in a teapot.*' The French version is '*une tempete dans un verre d'eau,*' which translates to 'a *storm in a glass of water.*' In the final analysis, a storm in a teacup is simply a situation in which people become irrationally angry about something that cannot be dignified with any appreciable degree of importance.

I walked out on that wonderful man. I left my beautiful home. The terrible insecurity I had brought over from my past life of trauma had come full circle to haunt me. Unknown to me, I had unconsciously developed severe trust issues. At a deep, subconscious level, I was unable to trust anyone. Unconsciously, I was unable to fully accept that anyone could ever care about me. Lurking somewhere at the back of my fractured psyche was the gnawing suspicion that there was always an ulterior motive behind any act of kindness towards me, and I believed that people were only ultimately out to hurt me. Because of this, I constantly had my guard up, even as I wallowed in my suspicions about everyone and everything around me. The only people I considered pure in my life were my children. The the only people that I genuinely felt connected to, and who I felt were a part of me, were my children and my God. Everything else in my life was tarnished.

As I could not trust anyone, my insecurities invariably led to severe fissures and difficulties in my marriage. If I had the opportunity to revisit my marriage, I would not leave such a wonderful husband. I would have understood that my husband was only trying to protect me. I would understand that he saw my vulnerability, and wanted to save me from it. Rather, my skewed interpretation of his good intentions was that he was jealous of me. I thought he did not want me to have a life. I thought he wanted to constrain me into a tiny corner, so that he could totally run my entire life as he saw fit. I thought he did not want me to be independent, and merely wanted me to remain under his thumb, and to do his bidding at all times. I thought he just wanted me to be his possession, and that he wanted to own me, lock, stock and barrel. My mind was totally corrupted, and so I could neither see straight nor think straight. I was totally incapable of evaluating people properly, and so my marriage fell apart at its seams.

My husband, very much like every other person in my life, simply would not allow me to walk away and live in peace. As far as he was concerned, if he couldn't have me, then no other person would. He proceeded to make my life a total nightmare. He showed up wherever I lived. Worse, he started to torment me by spreading false rumors about me. He told anyone who cared to listen that I was a lesbian. He literally branded me a prostitute, claiming that I had several men in my life. He went as far as showing up at my apartment to engage me in a vicious fight in which he attempted to take my children away from me. I found myself in a most untenable situation, and even though I know now that he truly loved me, and even though he has passed on, I have learnt to love him in my heart, in the realization that it was love that drove him to the extremes in which he uttered pronouncements that hurt me beyond the imaginable. Although his actions caused me so much pain, I still acknowledge that he did me more good than harm. He was always there if and whenever I reached out to him for help. In all honesty, Israel Sanchez was one of the best things that ever happened to me and my life.

The long and short of it all was that by my early twenties, I was already a single mother with two children. My saving grace was that I was educated. I had a college degree, in addition to a plethora of other degrees and certificates. Despite my seeming inadequacies, I literally had the world at my feet. I was a very beautiful woman. I had cultivated a regal carriage that magnetized people to me like steel to magnet. I had also learnt the proper social skills and graces, such that I took the commonplace acts of smiling and laughing to a whole new level of social ammunition to attract both admiration and goodwill. I had found out that when you are beautiful, you are automatically in demand. The world loves beautiful things and beautiful people. People go to church dressed up in their best finery. People go to work dressed up in their best formal attires. People go to parties all dressed up in beautiful designer wears. Beauty is simply an integral part of human nature. Beauty

110

is the one attribute that can conceal your pain. It can also take away your pain, and bring you joy and happiness. I started associating beauty with happiness, and that was what took me to the next chapter in my life; a chapter in which my commitment to beauty and fashion, and my association of beauty and fashion with happiness, would start to take the center stage in my life trajectory.

A new phase of my life had begun. It was at this stage that I met someone who would turn out to have one of the most remarkable influences on my life. She was an American woman, and a very beautiful woman for that matter, certainly one I considered one of God's angels on Earth. She recently passed in October of 2020 at the age of 96. This extraordinary woman became my rock, and I can safely declare that I probably owe virtually all I have become today to her. My circumstances, as at the time I met this woman, were entirely less than propitious, as I was swimming in very murky waters. I had just been separated from my husband. I was juggling my extremely difficult options with two babies on my hands. I was still in my early twenties in a strange land. In the comfort of my now defunct marriage, I had never had to work. I wasn't holding down a nine to five job. I didn't even know know how to travel in public transportation. Yet, I now had to learn to do all of these things in order to take care of my two babies.

Fate inexorably propelled me to a meeting with Miss Lucas. As soon as this woman saw me, it was as if she could see all my sorrow, and feel all my pain. Being the very wise, caring and thoughtful person that she was, she immediately felt compassionate towards me, and virtually completely adopted me to teach me how to live properly, how to be a proper mother to my children, and how to take proper care of myself. My fortuitous meeting with Miss Lucas inaugurated my lessons on being a fully functioning adult. She became my teacher, and my life coach. Before I met her, I was simply bumbling through life, and improvising by mimicking and implementing what I saw around me. I feebly attempted to separate the positive from the negative, and then mimic what I perceived to be positive, patterning myself after it. That meant, of course, that I had no real structure. Invariably, it also meant I was doing all the wrong things, which was the reason why my marriage fell apart in the first place. It was lack of both a well-adjusted mental and emotional structure that led me to stupidly leave my husband over a trivial issue, and why I did not go back. In retrospect, I think I was just looking for a reason to walk away. I was looking for a reason to be alone.

Obviously, I felt totally unworthy of being loved. I did not feel worthy of someone who could truly love me, and care about me. I felt that the idyllic setting of love and comfort that my husband freely and unconditionally gave me was all a cruel joke, and I wanted to leave before he left me. At a subconscious level, I seemed to believe that he would definitely leave me, as he was probably mistaken and misguided to think he could love a broken person like me. Clearly, I could never really come to terms with the fact that I was a person of some value, and a person of some importance. As they say, a tree is as strong as its roots, but if the tree has no roots, then that tree has no strength, and the tree will eventually fall. Many times, I felt like a tree without roots.

Miss Louise Lucas became my roots. I loved her dearly, and I will always celebrate her because she taught me how to be a real person. She taught me how to appreciate myself. She taught me how to love myself. She taught me how to love my children. She taught me how to love being alive. She taught me how to love all that life has on offer. I will remain eternally grateful to Louise Lucas, as today, I can not only feel my roots, but can actually see my roots. She gave me roots for growth, for strength, and for resilience. I now had a foundation for moving on to the next chapter of my life. I continued to educate myself. I continued to honor and hone my intellect. Finally, I can declare that honoring and honoring my intellect has kept my mind at that place in which my sanity has remained secure. I am filled with gratitude.

10

The Queen

"I am a queen, and I demand to be treated like a queen." - Sheila Jackson Lee, Member, US House of Representatives. Author, Juneteenth National Independence Day Act.

I was always a queen. Quite frankly, as far as I can recollect, even as a young girl, everything about me screamed *royalty*. I was regal in the way I carried myself. I was poised in my interactions with others. I was neat and immaculate in my dressing. Indeed, my entire being exuded an aura that stood me out amongst my peers. I easily recall how, as a little girl, as I stepped out, even for the most mundane of outings, people would tease me about the way I walked. More often than not, someone would accost me, and, hands on hips, would sashay up and down, ostensibly mimicking the way I strutted my imaginary catwalk, intoning, *"Here comes the queen! Here comes the queen!"* As I was still so young, I possibly did not really grasp the import of what they were trying to convey about me. I merely lapped up what I perceived to be compliments.

Being an avid reader, as I grew up I started to consume my own fair share of fairy tale novels. I took to those fantasy tales like fish to water. I read many tales that involved kings, queens, princes and princesses. Yet, they also involved witches and wicked stepmothers, to spice up the stories. Many of such tales were, more or less, of a tragic slant, but would invariably always have a happy ending. Indeed, all my fairy tales had happy endings. In fact, I doubt if a fairy tale is worth its name if it does not conclude with a happy ending. Fairy tales express hopes. In my extensive reading, I discovered that the story characters that bring about those miracles of hope varied from one story setting to another, as they are products of local belief systems that belong to tradition. Such traditions may contain imaginary elements, but also traces of factual history. I encountered fairies and goblins on the one hand, and wicked stepmothers on the other. Somewhere in between, the princesses that were my real heroines played their part, ably supported by chivalrous kings and princes. The history is, by itself, often an imagined one. For instance, King Arthur of England inspired romances that were carried into fairytale plots in which enchanted objects like swords, mirrors and cups held sway, while dangers from monsters and forests soaked the narrative with suspense. Fairy tales evoke every kind of violence, injustice, and mischance. Yet, it is the promise of a happy ending that ultimately justifies those tales of terrible and dark deeds.

I suppose, as I have already mentioned, I never really understood what those who teased me as a young girl meant by their chants of, *"Here comes the queen! Here comes the queen!"* Yet. I would soon gain an introduction into the world of the *beauty queen*, a world which, by the way, I truly belonged to. At the age of 18, I entered for my first beauty pageant, the Miss Guyana USA pageant, and I won the top prize to finally earn the name I had been called from childhood. I became *Miss Guyana USA*. In retrospect, I believe I knew I would win in that contest. I wanted to stand out. I wanted to be beautiful. I wanted to win. My combined commitment to that pageant, and the desire to win the contest, was merely reflective of all that I had desired all my life. In everything I did, I always wanted to be the best. My passion for winning was total. It was all-consuming.

I also recognized something else inside of me. It was a feeling of accomplishment that accompanied genuine and diligent preparation towards the achievement of a worthy objective. I had found my own niche, and my own formidable forte, in the world of beauty pageantry. I realized that the world literally worships at the feet of beauty. The world adores beauty. I was also keenly aware that the world associates beauty with royalty. That meant queens are supposed to be beautiful. The term *Beauty Queen* now made eminent sense to me. The attention, adulation and respect that came with the title of Miss Guyana USA was unbelievable. I suppose, even if only on the subconscious level, this was what I had always craved all my life. Finally, here I was, literally sitting in the middle of the cookie jar. That was how I felt. It was such an exhilarating feeling to be a beauty queen; to watch everyone jostling among themselves just to take a picture with you. Everyone also wanted to say hello to you, and to give you gifts. That night, I was inundated with gifts from the contest itself, and by people who attended the contest, and by other people who came to the contest because I was a participant, and who were simply elated that I won.

It was extremely impactful to be recognized as a beauty queen. Being a queen meant being beautiful in everything that I had been coached to be in preparing for the contest. Everything revolved around *beauty*. I was instructed on how to walk beautiful. I was instructed on how to talk beautiful. I was instructed on how to look beautiful. I was instructed on how to dress beautiful. Everything related to beauty. I became convinced that my earlier theory that the world simply worships beauty was perfectly valid after all. That conviction was the stepping stone to a lifelong venture.

I started my own beauty contest. I organized my first pageant. It was a local pageant, and it turned out exceedingly well. The truly remarkable thing that I could sense was that the participants at that pageant were experiencing the same feelings I had experienced at my own first beauty contest. I was excited. Most of the participants at that pageant were broken young women. Each and every one of those contestants was coming from a story of trauma, and they came to the pageant with all their warts and scars.

My eyes suddenly opened to a fresh insight. I seemed to have stumbled on a common denominator between *pain* and *beauty*. Incredible as it seemed, I started to see the connection between beauty and pain, and I started to study it. In essence, beauty seemingly has an ugly side to it, in the form of a story of trauma. Blissfully, however, people do not usually hear that ugly story, principally because the focus is always on the beauty. At this point, I came into conscious awareness of my own journey of pain and trauma. That awareness instantly bequeathed me a mission; a life mission. Henceforth, I was going to build on this insightful knowledge of the poignant nexus between beauty and pain.

The net result was that I became more engaged with looking beautiful, and surrounding myself with beautiful things. I became enamored with the pleasurable task of beautifying anything and everything within whispering distance of me. Beauty had transformed into my *magnificent obsession.* I formed a group of women who modeled with me. I enrolled myself in a school of design, so I could learn more and better professional ways of transforming anything and everything I touched into an item of beauty. I enrolled myself in a school of cosmetology to learn how to professionally apply makeup, and how to professionally style hair. I was literally intoxicated with my magnificent obsession as I became more and more involved in this new and totally consuming interest in beauty.

Very soon, it became obvious that I had started to attract the attention of people of high standing in society. In what seemed like a twinkling of an eye, I started getting proclamations, and receiving awards, citations and recognitions. I was inducted into the African-American Who's Who. I was inducted into the Madison Who's Who. I received proclamations and citations from the City of New York, the State of New York, and the government of the United States. I was inundated with invitations to attend functions that I hitherto could not attend because they were simply beyond my budgetary capacity, and most certainly, outside my own limited sphere of influence. I had to admit that beauty not only works, it also sells. I was having the time of my life. Unknown to me, I was about to meet a man who would later turn out one of the most remarkable influencers of my life journey.

At this stage in his remarkable career as a Hollywood actor and movie star, the man had become a powerful and influential United Nations humanitarian ambassador. Uniquely stepping out of his comfort zone as a serial award-winning movie screen idol, he was now doing so many extraordinary things on the global turf as a UNICEF ambassador. In detached terms, this man was no stranger to me as, by this time, I had already seen so many of his movies, and must have watched *"The Color Purple"* a dozen times. I was in attendance at an event at Carnegie Hall. Because I was a special guest, I was allowed backstage. The man was keynote speaker at the event, and his dressing room backstage had, not unnaturally, become a Mecca of sorts, as a crowd of admiring fans had gathered in his dressing room. At each break in the program, he came backstage for a brief intermission. At a point, I happened to be backstage, close to the dressing room of my friend, which was next to the man's dressing room. The man, Danny Glover, was already at the peak of his Hollywood career, and that day, he was the main attraction at that Carnegie Hall event.

My goddaughter, who was only nine years old at that time, was with me. Suddenly, she nudged me, and said, *"Auntie, Mr Glover is looking at you! Let us go over to him."* A thick crowd surrounded the man. As I had absolutely no intention of pushing my way through that crowd, I simply stood right there, waiting and hoping the crowd would thin out, but it never did. At some point, I looked up and caught his gaze. He winked at me. My little goddaughter was beside herself with excitement. Prancing up and down, she asked for my card. She took the card, and weaving her little body through the crowd, she arrived in front of the great actor, and gave him my card saying, *"My auntie wants your number."* He brought out his card and wrote his number on it, drawing a little heart next to it. *"Tell your auntie to call me after the event,"* he told her. A little while later, he suddenly materialized at my side. I don't quite remember how he got next to me, but there we were, standing next to each other. A photographer took a picture of us. To this day, I still have that picture.

I lived in Brooklyn. As I drove home in my cute little Mercedes, I decided to give his number a try, feeling quite certain that he might have given a fake number, not wanting a star-struck fan to constitute herself into a nuisance in his life. I called the number from my little cell phone. A recorded voice responded. That same recorded voice is still on Mr Glover's phone to this day. I hung up quickly. But I was understandably excited and scared all at the same time. I recall that this was in January of 2003. I rode on the crest of excitement all day. The next morning, at around 7am, as I was getting my young children ready for school, my phone rang. I was not accustomed to receiving phone calls that early in the day, since all my phone acquaintances knew only too well that, at that early hour, I would be in the throes of getting my brood ready for school.

"Yes?" I said, rather testily.

"Sanchez?"

"Danny Glover."

I can't even begin to describe how I felt. I literally broke into a celebratory dance.

"Morning," I finally managed to blurt out, trying to control my excitement.

"What are you doing today?"

"Well, for now I'm taking my children to school."

"I would like you to have lunch with me. I'm staying at the Millennium Plaza at the United Nations. I leave for Venezuela tonight. But I want you to have lunch with me today, so I can listen to your story."

My excitement can only be imagined. I couldn't believe this was happening to me. It was all like a dream from which I didn't want to awaken. It all seemed so unreal and surreal at the same time. The questions of incredulity ran through my mind. "Did Mr Danny Glover just call my phone. Did he just invite me to lunch? Did that famous movie star you see on the big screen just call me? It was all so unbelievable. A few hours later, I found myself at lunch with Mr Glover. At that time, I was carrying around an ambitious proposal to do a Miss CARICOM International Beauty Pageant. That pageant was my ultimate dream. I had done pageants in the past, but they had been on a smaller, and local level. Now, I was setting my sights higher. I had decided to move onto the international circuit. It was an ambitious aspiration, and I knew it. I had drawn up a draft model of the structure of the pageant. I took it with me anywhere I went. We are all familiar with the concept of putting one's plans down in clear and precise writing, so that it can seek manifestation in the material realm. That was my hope as, for six months, I went around with the concept paper for my dream pageant.

Then, the invitation to have lunch with Mr Glover came, one that, not even in my wildest dreams could I have ever envisaged. Of course, as I ambled through the lobby of The Millenium Hotel, my concept note was carefully tucked away in my handbag. On arrival at his suite, I sat down like a scared little rabbit, watching as this giant of a man who towered over me kept walking back and forth, a phone in one hand, and another phone in his ears, even as the hotel phone kept ringing. There was a messenger at the door delivering scripts. His hotel suite was a madhouse. I sat there wondering what I was doing in this place. He had sandwiches, water, sprite and hot tea on the table. I opted for some tea and a sandwich, yet I was too agitated to drink or eat. I could hardly breathe. I couldn't believe I was sitting there watching this man, standing at 6 feet 3 inches tall.

"How tall are you, lady." He asked.

"I am 5 feet, three inches."

"My daddy would have loved you. My daddy was a little man. My mama towered over him. He was such a little man, but she loved that man to distraction."

Mr Glover talked about his family, and about himself. In between his intelligent chatter, he would talk to people on the phone about scripts, and then he would get back to me.

"What do you want with me?" He finally asked.

My pageant concept note sprang into my hand.

I gave it to him. He glanced at it.

"Okay, I will read it when I get a chance, and get back to you, but you need to know that I don't do pageants."

"Lend your name to it," I replied quickly.

He stared at me for a second .

"What do you mean by 'lend my name to it'?"

"I want you to attach your name to it. That means you endorse it. That alone will attract sponsors, and that would help me make this concept a reality."

"I'm traveling in a couple hours. I will read it as soon as I get a chance."

I gave him the proposal. A couple of hours later, his driver arrived to take him to the airport, and I left. All the way home, I kept pinching myself to make sure I wasn't dreaming. I still couldn't believe I had sat for four hours talking to Mr Danny Glover. I still couldn't believe I had actually handed over my proposal to Mr Danny Glover. Clearly, fate had seen fit to smile kindly upon me.

Two days later, again around 7:00am in the morning, my phone rang. It was Mr Glover .

"Sanchez," he said, *"what do you want me to do?"*

"Just permit me to use your name. Allow me to attach your name and your personality to my pageant. That is all I ask. I am asking you to be my destiny helper."

There was silence at the other end. My heart was in my mouth. Finally, the man spoke.

"Alright. You have it. Whatever it is that you want from me, you have it. Go ahead. I'm with you. You have my best wishes for a brilliant and wonderful pageant."

My knees buckled under me, and I almost collapsed. I burst into tears of relief and joy. That was the beginning of my wonderful journey with Miss CARICOM International Foundation, and Miss CARICOM International Pageant. I met Mr Glover in January of 2003, and in July of 2004, my dream became a reality.

Mr Danny Glover was, and has remained my destiny helper. There are certain degrees or dimensions of greatness that you alone cannot attain all by yourself. Destiny helpers are men and women positioned by God to bring into fulfillment your plans, and your purpose. You can never get to a certain point in life without destiny helpers.

Some of people are laboring in life without attaining their desired result because they have not connected with their destiny helpers. Destiny helpers are very important to succeeding in life. They make your success much easier than you could ever imagine. If you were to work on your own it might take you years to accomplish your goals, but with your destiny helper it can take you less than a week. Our prayers and heart desire should simply be, *"Lord, connect me to my destiny helper."*

It is God alone that raises men and women. But He does it through other men and women. The help that you are looking for is in the hand of someone else. Your ability to identify, embrace, value, appreciate, locate and celebrate the people that God has assigned to help you is critical to the fulfillment of your destiny. A lot of people struggle through life, not because they lack skills or talent, but because they have not discovered their destiny helpers. There is no man on Earth that is self-made. The journey to destiny fulfilment will always place a very high demand on the input of people that are critical to our destination. Many people are not achieving their highest potential because certain relationships are not in place in their lives. By a similar token, those who are fulfilled in their aspirations seem to have certain beneficial relationships in their lives.

Destiny connectors are the people that have the connections and contacts that are critical to your destiny fulfilment. They are your ultimate connectors. They can connect you in a way that your degree and certificate would not be able to in your life-time. These are special relationships that can open doors in a moment, which your degrees and skills won't open in a lifetime. I have observed that there is a strong connection between the quality of your relationships and the opportunities that you will be exposed to in life.

Destiny mentors are the people that have the experience and exposure that you need to fulfil your destiny. The truth of life is that if you want to go further, get a mentor. Mr Glover has been, not just my destiny helper, but also my destiny mentor. Isaac Newton once said, *"If I have seen farther than others, it is because I was standing on the shoulders of giants."* Behind every successful person, there was a mentor who helped them along the way. Some of the most influential people in history were encouraged to succeed by some of the most well-known people of their time. Socrates mentored Plato, Plato mentored Aristotle, and Aristotle mentored Alexander the great. Thomas Edison mentored Henry Ford. Steve Jobs was mentored by William Hewlett, one of the Co-founders of the HP company. Oprah Winfrey was mentored by celebrated author and poet, the late Maya Angelou. Former Apple CEO, the late Steve Jobs, was mentor to Facebook CEO, Mark Zuckerberg.

Destiny sponsors are the people that God has ordained to fund your dreams. The vision that God has committed to your hand cannot be funded by your 9 to 5 job. The money that you need to sustain the project that God has committed to your hand is not in heaven, it is in someone else's account. Today, I remain eternally grateful to those who saw sufficient merit in the Miss CARICOM International Pageant to sponsor it. I have also had what I call destiny recommendations from people who have spoken well,of me and my capabilities in places where my own voice could not be heard. You must surround yourself with people who will mention your name in a room full of opportunities. Knowing people that can recommend you for the right places will always give you a significant edge in life. In sacrosanct truth, everything you've ever wanted in life is a relationship away. It is not enough to have talent and skills; you must understand the power of building valuable relationships. Jim Rohn once said, *"You must constantly ask yourself these questions: Who am I around? What are they doing to me? What have they got me reading? What have they got me saying? Where do they have me going? What do they have me thinking? And most important, what do they have me becoming? Then ask yourself the big question – Is this ok?"* Ultimately, although the journey to destiny fulfilment will require passion, self-discovery, gifts, talents and hard work, it is not *what* you have in your life, but *who* you have in your life, that counts. The core secret of great people is that they work hard at building great relationships. Money can be spent quickly, but relationships are inexhaustible.

Mr Glover kept faith with his endorsement. He allowed me to use, not only his name, but also his combined person and personality. My dream became a reality in July of 2004. Miss CARICOM International Foundation was inaugurated at the secretariat of the Republic of Guyana. I also produced and anchored a magnificent pageant. Mr Glover traveled to Guyana with my delegation. The government of Guyana not only accorded my team a wonderful reception, but also totally embraced my program. There is no gainsaying the fact that Mr Glover's presence made all the difference. Guyana's business sector welcomed the man with open arms. The government was entranced by him. Without doubt, God was on my side as I performed the greatest public relations stunt of my entire life. Mr Glover ate our local pepper pot. He visited the market. He visited the bauxite district. He visited the phone company, the power company, and the rum company. He was honored with the key to the city of Georgetown. All in all, Mr Glover was well received and entertained by the people of Guyana. That was hardly surprising. He is such a warm and caring human being who, in all truth, is also one of the greatest humanitarians that I know till this day.

We remain very close friends and colleagues to this day. He has since traveled with me to South Africa, Guyana, Trinidad, Antigua, Montserrat and many parts of America. He has supported all that we do. He is a staunch supporter of gender equality and the rights of women and girls. This wonderful relationship with Mr Glover has seen him commissioning Miss CARICOM international to give an award in his name. It is called the Danny Glover Power of Dreams Award, and it is awarded to people who follow their dreams, and in doing so leave a positive impact on a person, place or thing. Today, I am proud to say there have been many recipients of this award, including distinguished persons like a First Lady of Nigeria, First Ladies of Guyana, several Kings, the presidents of some countries, and so many unsung heroes in many communities globally. it is considered an extreme honor to receive the Danny Glover Power of Dreams Award because it was created in the image of what Mr Glover represents as a global humanitarian who supports the United Nations in its fight for the rights of people who can't fight for themselves, and as someone who has committed himself to the empowerment and promotion of ordinary citizens all over the world. As an icing on our cake of blessings, Miss CARICOM International Foundation now also has the commission to give out the United States of America Presidential Volunteer Service Award. At this stage in my evolution, my mission is to make everyone feel royal. My mission is also to continue to promote all that is beautiful, noble and praiseworthy about our global family.

11

My United Nations Connection

"I am here to say it loud and clear. The United Nations stands with women and girls everywhere. Women and girls will not be silenced. Their demands for their rights and freedoms echo around the globe." - UN Secretary-General António Guterres. The Commission on the Status of Women (CSC). March 6, 2023

The United Nations, referred to informally as the UN, is an intergovernmental organization whose stated purposes are to maintain international peace and security, develop friendly relations among nations, achieve international cooperation, and serve as a centre for harmonizing the actions of nations. It is the world's largest international organization. The UN is headquartered in New York City, but maintains satellite offices in Geneva, Vienna, Nairobi, and The Hague, where the International Court of Justice is head. The UN was established after World War II with the aim of preventing future world conflicts, and actually started off as the League of Nations. On April 25, 1945, fifty nations met in San Francisco to draft the UN charter, which was adopted on June 25, 1945. The charter took effect on October 24, 1945, when the UN began operations. As defined by its charter, the organization's objectives include maintaining international peace and security, protecting human rights, delivering humanitarian aid, promoting sustainable development, and upholding international law. At its founding in 1945: the UN had 51 member states, and as of 2023, it has 193 member states, almost all of the world's sovereign nations.

The UN System is composed of a multitude of specialized agencies, funds, and programs, including the World Bank Group, the World Health Organization (WHO), the World Food Program, UNESCO, and UNICEF. Additionally, various non-governmental organizations have been granted consultative status with the Economic and Social Council and other agencies. The UN's chief administrative officer is the secretary general, currently Portuguese politician and diplomat António Guterres, who began his first five year-term on January 1, 2017, and was re-elected for a second term June 8, 2021. The organization is financed with voluntary contributions from its member states.

I was introduced to the UN in the early eighties. Some friends of mine introduced me to an entity that was lobbying certain countries for the execution of infrastructure projects. The job entailed securing funds outside the purview of the World Bank. Essentially, therefore, it meant networking with diplomats, and especially getting the attention of the ambassadors of those countries, on the one hand, and lobbying those companies that were in the business of loaning money for infrastructure programs in African countries, on the other hand. In the course of all these diplomatic forays, I received many invitations to attend quite a few events at the United Nations, and the Millennium Hotel. I embarked on several trips to Washington DC to meet with ambassadors and heads of state to lobby these interests. As it happened, the more exposed I was to these circles, the more I seemed to develop an affinity for the United Nations. I found myself cultivating a rather refreshing sort of fascination for the different countries, their peoples, culture, ways of life, and languages. I was particularly intrigued by, and drawn towards the continent of Africa. All the 17 Sustainable Development Goals of the UN seemed to strike at the very heart of the core needs of the people of Africa. The 2030 Agenda for Sustainable Development adopted by all United Nations Member States in 2015 provides a shared blueprint for peace and prosperity for people and the planet, now and into the future. At its heart are the 17 Sustainable Development Goals (SDGs), which are an urgent call for action by all countries, developed and developing, in a global partnership. They recognize that ending poverty and other deprivations must go hand-in-hand with strategies that improve health and education, reduce inequality, and spur economic growth, all the while tackling climate change and working to preserve our oceans and forests.

Africa, in particular, appeared to reflect the need to vigorously fight poverty, hunger, lack of education, gender inequality, lack of health care and dereliction of the environment. In my perception, it seemed as if anytime these issues were discussed, it was, to all intents and purposes, about African people and their struggles. I saw myself as a victim of this discrimination, and since I was left with little choice than to be a part of the solution, I figured that becoming deeply involved with side work at the United Nations was my best recourse for making any significant impact. My involvement with the UN also provided an attractive opportunity to broaden my intellectual horizons, and to deepen my knowledge about a world beyond my current limited exposure. My journey to an uncommon attachment to the UN had started.

I wanted to be a part of the magnificent structure that housed the heart of operations of the diplomatic behemoth called the United Nations. As my interest grew, so did my education and information about the United Nations. In the process, I learned all about the UN concept of *consultative status*, and that my own organization could actually become intimately connected to the UN through a consultative status, and operate under the umbrella of credibility afforded by an affiliation with the UN. I became quite excited about this prospect, and commenced my path of application for a consultative status for my organization right away. The day my application was approved will easily rank as the happiest day of my life up to that point. I felt a sense of accomplishment that is difficult to express in words. My interpretation of

127

my new status was that I was now connected to the world as, to me, the UN was fully representative of the world. I started to gather all the information I could about the UN, its purpose, its functions and its functionalities. Today, I can safely boast that I have emerged a complete repository of information, if not a consummate custodian of encyclopedic knowledge about all those programs that are a reflection of the interests and needs of the people of the world as visible through the windows of the United Nations. I found out all I could about UNESCO, in the process discovering an opportunity to join UNESCO clubs. That was how I arrived at the UNESCO Institute of Fashion Education. I found I could accomplish so much by working with the 17 Sustainable Development Goals of the UN. I will attempt a lucid synopsis of these goals, with some emphasis on those aspects that appeal strongly to my own mission.

- Goal 1. End poverty in all its forms everywhere
- Goal 2. End hunger, achieve food security and improved nutrition and promote sustainable agriculture
- Goal 3. Ensure healthy lives and promote well-being for all at all ages. This is associated with a target to reduce global maternal morality rate, and prevent the deaths of newborns and children. It also targets diseases such as malaria, AIDS and other communicable disease, and the prevention and treatment of substance abuse, deaths from traffic accidents, a universal access to sexual and reproductive health care, the achievement of universal health coverage, and a reduction in the number of deaths and illness from hazardous chemicals and pollution. Women and girls around the world face major health challenges, and the commission on sustainable development considered health as a cross-cutting issue that addresses the fact that human beings are entitled to a healthy and productive life in harmony with nature, and that the goals of sustainable development SDG can only be achieved in the absence of a high prevalence of deliberating disease, while securing a healthy plan for the whole population requires poverty eradication.

- Goal 4. Ensure inclusive and equitable quality education and promote lifelong learning opportunities for all. The only was to eradicate poverty, and to protect and promote the health of human beings is to provide gainful employment, for which you must have an education, and in order to gain employment, you must be treated fairly and equally.

- Goal 5. Achieve gender equality and empower all women and girls. I am a woman today, and I was a girl a few years back. Since the UN was created, gender equality has been one of its main focal points. The *Commission on The Status of Women* (CSC), dedicated to the promotion of gender equality and the empowerment of women, has secured various landmark agreements, such as the Geneva Convention, in relation of all forms of discrimination against women, and the Beijing Declaration, a platform for action on the 66th Session of the General Assembly held in September 2011. The United Nations Secretary General at that time Ban Ki-Moon, on the occasion of the General Debate of the 66th Session of the General highlighted in his Report, "We the Peoples," *"the crucial role of gender equality as driver of development progress, recognizing that the potential of women had not been fully realized, owing to, inter alia, persistent social, economic and political inequalities. Gender inequalities are still deep-rooted in every society. Women suffer from lack of access to decent work and face occupational segregation and gender wage gaps. In many situations, they are denied access to basic education and health care and are victims of violence and discrimination. They are under-represented in political and economic decision-making processes. With the aim of better addressing these challenges and to identify a single recognized driver to lead and coordinate UN activities on gender equality issues, UN Women was established in 2010. UN Women works for the elimination of discrimination against women and girls, empowerment of women, and achievement of equality between women and men as partners and beneficiaries of development, human rights, humanitarian action and peace and security. The vital role of women and the need for their full and equal participation and leadership in all areas of sustainable development was reaffirmed in the Future We Want, as well as in the Open Working Group Proposal for Sustainable Development Goals. The proposed*

Sustainable Development Goal 5 addresses this and reads "Achieve gender equality and empower all women and girls."

- Goal 6. Ensure availability and sustainable management of water and sanitation for all.
- Goal 7. Ensure access to affordable, reliable, sustainable and modern energy for all.
- Goal 8. Promote sustained, inclusive and sustainable economic growth, full and productive employment and decent work for all.
- Goal 9. Build resilient infrastructure, promote inclusive and sustainable industrialization and foster innovation.
- Goal 10. Reduce inequality within and among countries.
- Goal 11. Make cities and human settlements inclusive, safe, resilient and sustainable.
- Goal 12. Ensure sustainable consumption and production patterns.
- Goal 13. Take urgent action to combat climate change and its impacts.
- Goal 14. Conserve and sustainably use the oceans, seas and marine resources for sustainable development.
- Goal 15. Protect, restore and promote sustainable use of terrestrial ecosystems, sustainably manage forests, combat desertification, and halt and reverse land degradation and halt biodiversity loss.
- Goal 16. Promote peaceful and inclusive societies for sustainable development, provide access to justice for all and build effective, accountable and inclusive institutions at all levels.
- Goal 17. Strengthen the means of implementation and revitalize the global partnership for sustainable development.

These are the sustainable development goals for the 2030 agenda adopted by all UN member state in 2015, and they share a blueprint for peace and prosperity for people and the planet, now and into the future. SDG goals arrested my attention. I am interested in people and our planet. My motto is CIP; *Caring Interest in People.* The SDGs speak into my own agenda. It was almost as if the SDGs were my own thoughts adopted wholesale by 178 countries. I dug my feet in, and decided that this was going to be my home. The UN was going to be my home. I was going to work with the SDGs, and help as many people as I could. My focus is gender-based. My passion for marginalized and rural people would push me to a place I never thought I would go to.

I will start with *poverty*. Poverty is connected to me in many more ways than one. I was homeless at the age of 9. Not only was I acutely aware of my state of poverty, I was also aware of some of the causes and effects of poverty. Child marriage is a celebrated cause of poverty. My mother was only 12 when she gave birth to me, with absolutely no foundation, no support, no role model, no education, and no leadership template. In such disenfranchising circumstances, how can one possibly avoid poverty and its debilitating effects? Society, and the very structure of that society, determines the economic status of the people. How can you possibly avoid marginalization and disenfranchisement if you are poor? Not unnaturally, good health and well-being can never be a part of your own personal dynamics if you are poor. As long as you are in abject poverty, and you are hungry, it is a mere matter of the inevitable that your health and well-being will be compromised. For you, also, quality education cannot be part of the equation of a balanced life. How can quality education co-exist with poverty and hunger? Without optimal health and well-being, you cannot possibly aspire to the next SDG, which is Goal 5; gender equality. Indeed, SDG goals 1,2,3, and 4 have tremendous bearing on the actualization of SDG 5. Women and girls are at the core of the principles underpinning the first four goals. Girls are bait for sexual predators, and because of those sexual implications, girls are a targeted gender. Young girls are either married off early, molested, abused, raped, given away, or sold because of sexuality. These were the reasons why gender equality simply had to be the core focus of all of my entire existence, and my commitment to the 17 SDG Goals of the UN. My mother, who was not educated, and who was exposed to abject poverty, had me at the age of 12. That could happen only because there was no gender protection, no foundation, and no support structure in place in her country. Society let her down. Her parents let her down. Leadership must remain under an inalienable obligation to protect their citizens. Laws and rules must be enacted to ensure a healthy environment for citizens. It is the non-negotiable responsibility of government to provide protection by instituting legislation and appropriate punishment for violations of those laws, such that citizens can live without fear, and focus on pursuing the natural life that entails the natural progression of growth from childhood into young adulthood, and into adulthood, and in full knowledge that they will only be exposed to issues that are related to those age milestones. This was decidedly not the case in my life, or in my mother's life, as in Guyana, the country of my birth, racial discrimination fueled by social dislocations that were encouraged by politics and government insensitivity resulted in the unwholesome atmosphere and temperature of my young life.

I often daydream as I sit in the General Assembly Hall at UN Headquarters, attending programs and listening to world leaders agree on resolutions that affect citizens all over the world. I would see myself sitting there, and making decisions that would protect women and children worldwide, in full consciousness of my personal motto of Caring Interest in People (CIP). Indeed, people have always been the centerpiece of my motivation. That was how MISS CARICOM International Foundation and CIP Inc. came to life. This would be the vehicle I would use to change the world. Indeed, I envisioned a more peaceful, safe and productive world where people can live with one another in peace, love and harmony. I have always felt like a royal personage. For those who believe in the afterlife in which the soul is reincarnated, I can safely say that, if my soul even remotely existed in the past, it must have existed as royalty. As far back as I can recall, my behavior was always reminiscent of nobility. I always carried myself with a regality borne of premium breeding, and an exposure to the finer things of life. I easily recall how, as a child, I had only one set of clothing as school uniform. I would wash my uniform, and set the pleats of my skirt as if it was being ironed. I would spread my little beddings over it, and lay on it to sleep at night. The result, of course, was that the pleats would set properly, and the skirt itself would seem as if it had been ironed. I wanted to look smart and neat at all times. My hair was always well braided. If, as a homeless child totally lacking in security, my appearance was always immaculate, you can only imagine how I am turned out now at the United Nations, where on near-daily basis, I am exposed to heads of states, kings and queens. In these days that I spend considerable amounts of time speaking with ambassadors, and having cups of tea with all these dignitaries, my reality has finally been realized, with the feeling of royalty growing stronger by the day.

My work with my foundation is so impactful that it attracts tremendous attention from women all over the world. These are all women like myself who seek to make a difference, and who, for one reason or the other, have cultivated the selfless desire to do something to improve the conditions of women worldwide, and because of this, my network of colleagues has grown to such an expansive magnitude that I find myself working with women from Nigeria, Sierra Leone, The Gambia, Ghana, Venezuela, Panama, Guyana, Liberia, Jamaica, Trinidad, Barbados, Antigua and a host of other countries as far flung from me as my imagination can conceive. My commitment and love for Africa and my colleagues in these African countries totally dominate my interest and motivation, even as reserve a sincere desire to see firsthand how life is in those countries. To that end, I have had the rare privilege of traveling to sixty eight countries in the process of promoting my work with Miss CARICOM International Foundation. I have also transformed into a role model of sorts to a lot of women, because of which I started helping other women to establish foundations that can contribute to the enormous of making the world a better place for women and girls. Many men have also become enamored with the idea of being a part of the global movement that is creating a better world for girls and women, and many of them have joined my network, so much so that the movement has seemingly taken on a life of its own. Our visibility and outreach is so remarkable that we have been able to teach essential life skills to girls and women. Such life skills include baking, hat making, marketing of small goods, sewing, cooking, crochet making, and carving of arts and crafts. As I have discovered, all these women needed was just someone to come in and teach them, organize them in a professional manner, and certify them so that the world can respect them.

All these I have been able to achieve under the auspices of my commission, UNESCO Institute of Fashion Education. We have been able to train and certify many women in life skills, enabling them to gain employment. In essence, we have empowered them to feel accomplished, and to be independent. This, most certainly, is what the SDGs is all about. Ultimately, if one can be sufficiently independent and accomplished to adequate take care of one's family, one has succeeded in validating the aim of the UN SDGs. I am immensely proud of my work with the UN, as at each session of the Commission on the Status of Women (CSC), I have earned the privilege of issuing both a written statement and a verbal statement that the United Nations publishes to highlight our work, and our commitment to the status of women worldwide. To date, we have over a dozen published written and verbal statements in the UN Network. In the circumstances, I can only declare with understandable pride an$ satisfaction that my involvement with the United Nations has proved to be the principal driving force in my commitment to the improvement in the quality of life of women and girls, including myself. I have become tremendously empowered in both intellect and knowledge. My exposure to the stories of thousands of women at the United Nations has inspired me to write my own story.

Indeed, the United Nations remains very impactful in my life. I have been accorded the rare privilege of personally breaking bread with several world leaders. They have also given me valuable insights into the peculiarities incident to their leadership of their various countries. I have assisted in highlighting and addressing issues facing women and girls, and how to provide a better quality of life for them in these countries. There is no doubt that without my UN connection, I couldn't possibly be privy to all the information, education and experience that is now at my disposal in the area of the marginalization of women and girls, and I certainly wouldn't have been able to contribute as much as I done in that field. Some of the women I have encountered on this journey have left a lasting impression on me, and some of these women are still in my life. Amongst them is a remarkable woman from Nigeria, Dr Ada Menakaya, a very intelligent lady whose story touched me so much that I have remained closely connected to her. To this day, the passion she deploys to sharing her education and work for a better quality of life for girls and women is shared by me. I feel very strongly about these issues because of my own story, of course.

As might be expected, along the journey, I have met a few women who sought to sow a seed of doubt in me by querying why I am so committed to the mission of empowering women and girls. There are also women that I took under my wings, mentoring them to become established personalities in their own right, and teaching them how to read and write properly, all in a bid to broaden their horizons, create arresting profiles for them, and establish credible identities for them, only for them to turn around to betray my trust in them by clandestinely seeking to undermine my efforts and activities. I have resolutely refused to be discouraged by their disingenuous and underhand conduct. As long as I keep getting at least 51% returns on my commitment to this journey, I will remain faithful to that commitment, especially since I now know only too well that so many women just need a helping hand, while many others just want to be told they can do it, *"this is the way to do it, and I will be there to help you to do it."* In their gratitude, they are ever so willing to go out and help other women, such that every woman I've helped in turn helps other women, and the cycle continues in such a manner as to create the reality of thousands of women being helped to find a new purpose for living. That reward in faithful commitment to the overall mission; one that, wittingly or unwittingly, has now turned into a *train-the-trainer* mission, is so priceless and gracious that I will sustain the pursuit of that mission until I take my last breath on this Earth. Ultimately, the United Nations will always be part of my world if only because the United Nations is the world.

12

Journey Back To My Roots

"Return to the root and you will find the meaning." - Jianzhi Sengcan

I had left my Guyana homeland with nothing but memories of abuse, bitterness and tragedy, and embarked on the very uncertain journey to start a new life in a faraway land, clueless as to what lay ahead of me. That journey finally brought me to the United States, land of the free and the brave and, for me, a land of hope that would yet turn out a repository of endless opportunities. As I would later discover, the United States is truly *"the Land of the Free,"* because here anyone is entitled to stand up for the values that matter to them. It is also the *"Home of the Brave,"* because there are people here who are willing to stand up for causes that resonate with them without regard for their popularity. I will take the trouble to render on these pages the lyrics of the Star-Spangled Banner, the national anthem of the United States of America, and where those two powerful phrases are housed.

O! say can you see by the dawn's early light,
What so proudly we hailed at the twilight's last gleaming,
Whose broad stripes and bright stars through the perilous fight,
O'er the ramparts we watch'd, were so gallantly streaming?

And the Rockets' red glare, the Bombs bursting in air,
Gave proof through the night that our Flag was still there;
O! say does that star-spangled Banner yet wave,
O'er the Land of the free and the home of the brave?

On the shore dimly seen through the mists of the deep,
Where the foe's haughty host in dread silence reposes,
What is that which the breeze, o'er the towering steep,
As it fitfully blows, half conceals, half discloses?
Now it catches the gleam of the morning's first beam,
In full glory reflected now shines on the stream,
'Tis the star-spangled banner, O! long may it wave
O'er the land of the free and the home of the brave.

And where is that band who so vauntingly swore
That the havoc of war and the battle's confusion,
A home and a country should leave us no more?
Their blood has washed out their foul footsteps pollution.
No refuge could save the hireling and slave,
From the terror of flight, or the gloom of the grave,
And the star-spangled banner in triumph doth wave,
O'er the Land of the Free and the Home of the Brave.

O! thus be it ever, when freemen shall stand,
Between their lov'd home and the war's desolation,
Blest with vict'ry and peace, may the Heav'n rescued land,
Praise the Power that hath made and preserv'd us a nation!
Then conquer we must, when our cause it is just,
And this be our motto – "In God is our Trust;"
And the star-spangled Banner in triumph shall wave,
O'er the Land of the Free and the Home of the Brave.

Yes, indeed, I found my last bastion of hope in the United States, and I started living the *American dream*. The United States quickly became my new home, and now, raising myself within the context of American traditions, culture and mannerisms, I found myself gradually becoming alienated and disconnected from any fundamental semblance of my Guyanese identity. Yet, in later years, fueled by knowledge, education and information I had gained as an American citizen and an American-educated woman, and against the background of my exposure to the United Nations Sustainable Development Goals, I gradually grew into the sober realization that the citizens of Guyana, especially the women of Guyana, needed me. This renewed sense of discovery, and the acute sentiment of national consciousness, inexorably propelled me to embark on a journey of transformation, to rediscover my source, to reclaim my roots, and to reconnect with a land filled with many young people just like me who were suffering as I had, with no one to help, and with seemingly no hope of redemption. I recalled that I once questioned the existence of God, and if He did exist, why he wasn't keeping His word to protect the little children. Now, with a better understanding of God, and how He intervenes in the affairs of Man, and backed by the conviction that He does not come down to act on behalf of His children, but rather sends His appointed messengers on that vital mission, I finally arrived at the realization that I had to go back home, and let them know that there is, indeed, a God, but that Man was the problem.

I had barely managed to survive my early years in the country of my birth. Even that token of grace was made possible only because I was given a helping hand by a few people, and now that I had found strength for purposeful living, and discovered a new and authentic identity in my new land, America, I was prepared to go back and fight for those who, just like me, were barely surviving on the fringes of humanity. Despite the circumstances that led me to relocate to the United States, the bottom line was that I survived, and was granted the opportunity to receive premium education. In fact, my assimilation into American culture had been so exhilarating that I was all but blissfully distracted from any thought of maintaining my Guyanese heritage. The core insight, however, that I did not lose sight of was that this land; the land of America, highlighted the positive aspects of a life of freedom, and that human rights non-negotiably entailed having a proper childhood, and being nurtured into normal adulthood, in the full protection and safety of a state that guaranteed access to education and security, as a fundamental human right, and not as a privilege, and that everyone was entitled to this right.

As my passion to reconnect with my country of birth grew stronger, I began to truly long for home, and to reconnect with my mother and siblings. By this time, Miss CARICOM Foundation, and its affiliated Miss CARICOM International Pageant, was no longer a mere dream, but had transformed into a reality. All that I had experienced up until now was eminently validated by this new venture, and I could now make my mother proud and happy, knowing she had produced a princess, and one who, not only had survived the vicissitudes of life, but now understood and appreciated her mother's journey as a child that had had a child. I was now in a position to feel my mother's pain, sorrow and numbness, and her disconnectedness with a world that had broken her heart, and dashed her hopes. I could now try to reach out to her, with the purpose of reconnecting her to that world, and show her that the sun could still bring laughter to her lips, and that the moon could still brighten her darkest night with its soft and iridescent glow. I was filled with the anticipation of hugging my mother, and taking her out to lunch, and having a relationship with her all over again.

At this point, I hasten to mention that I had previously sponsored my mother to come to America, but at the due date of her appointment, she couldn't be found, and that was how that opportunity was lost. Without further waste of time, I engaged my friend, Patsy, to help me plan and execute a vacation trip for my mother that would entail my friend bringing my mother out of Guyana to Trinidad for a few days. It turned out a successful venture. I recall how excited she was to ride on an escalator for the first time in her life. At that time, I was employed as a New York state correction officer, and had planned my two-week vacation such that I could join my friend and my mother in Barbados, where I had made all the arrangements for her to stay for a few months. Patsy had volunteered to travel with her, and keep her safe, and all I had to do was offset all the expenses for both of them to travel. All was going well, and I was truly happy.

I arrived Barbados to find my mother in what must have been the happiest I had ever seen her, at least as far as I could remember. She was relaxed and filled with joy, and the light of delight I saw in her face was as awesome as it was incredible. I cannot fully express the emotions that I felt at that moment. Yet, I tried to remain calm, as I did not want to ignite an emotional outburst from my mother. I recall thanking God over and over again until it became a chorus in my spirit. I simply could not stop saying, *"Thank you Lord for this blessed and beautiful day."* However, as might be expected with the average fairy tale, barely halfway into that carefully orchestrated trip, my mother became consumed with the emotional rollercoaster of going back and forth between her past and her present. She simply broke down, and it became clear that she could neither face nor understand her current state of happiness. I remain at a loss as to what caused her disintegration, or what conflicting feelings caused her to reject happiness. It suddenly transformed into a very painful and traumatic time, as my mother chose to find every excuse to hurt me emotionally. At that time, I did not understand that this was a *protective reaction,* since all she had previously known was pain, sorrow, abuse and disappointment. What she was now experiencing appeared too good to be true. In any case, why should this time be any different? Therefore, her only sane recourse was to *mess it up before it messed her up.* I had to return to work, as my vacation had come to an end, and left Patsy with her to continue the vacation. Unfortunately, my friend became so afraid of all the threats from my mother that the vacation had to be brought to an abrupt end, and my friend and my mother returned to Guyana, making my joy at her happiness sadly short lived.

Soon enough, another opportunity for reconnection made its appearance. This would be another chance to bond with my mother, and perhaps we would make a success of the opportunity this time around. My hopes were, once again, heightened at the prospect of meeting her on a new platform. You see, by now I was riding on the euphoric crest of success and popularity. I had now fully transformed into royalty. I was now the irrepressibly beautiful, educated, elegant, charming and sophisticated Dr Monica Sanchez. Matters could not have been otherwise. I was a cherished protégé of Hollywood icon and UN-UNDP Ambassador, Mr Danny Glover, a big screen idol who was supporting all the good causes, such as HIV-AIDS, Children, Creative Arts, Environment, Health, Homelessness, Human Trafficking, Human Rights, Ocean, Poverty, Slavery and many others.

Yet, my new hope and desire for rapprochement with my mother would be only short lived. Matters simply did not materialize as I had hoped. I did go back home to Guyana. I did have the most fabulous, and the most exhilaratingly successful event ever held in Guyana. Mine had become a household name in Guyana. The whole country knew my name, and a face that was emblazoned on billboards all across Guyana, to the accompaniment of the well-known visage of Danny Glover. I was accorded a royal welcome by the government of Guyana, at that time headed by Dr Bharrat Jagdeo, then President of the Republic of Guyana. Without doubt, my triumphant entry into my homeland of Guyana in that month of July 2004, was both an epochal, and a historic event. Sadly, in what must pass as the most monumentally tragic event of my life, my mother would not witness my moment of glory, and the moment of biggest promotion of my life, as her own life came to an abrupt end in August of 2003, a year earlier, at the tender age of 57 years old. She died of a heart attack. As usual, this was yet another bitter sweet moment of my life, reiterating the fact that good and bad, negative and positive, bitter and sweet, all seem to be Siamese twins in our life journey, and this was a reality I had to learn to cope with.

The loss of my mother had a tremendous impact on me. I suddenly became filled with a burning desire to do more in the areas of *children having children,* and existence in a society that does not do enough to protect the vulnerable.

I started to embrace my new identity of an advocate fighting for the rights of people, especially women and girls. My journey back to Guyana, and the epochal events that attended that trip, was the fire that I needed to propel me to where I am now at the United Nations, fighting for marginalized and rural communities worldwide. Miss CARICOM Foundation now has booths on the ground in over nine countries, and has trained and certified over 250,000 people in life skills such as cooking, cake baking, hat making, sewing, farming, domestic cleaning, and other such vocations under the auspices of our commission, UNESCO Institute of Fashion Education, with the bulk of those graduates being Nigerians, thanks to our committed partnership with Save African Children on Social Vices Initiative, Dr Jeff Ramsey and his lovely wife.

I can safely declare that the impact my journey back home to my roots, and the relearning of my native culture, and how all that has fostered a deeper connection to who I really am, will remain the true essence of who I will continue to be. My roots, and the genuine efforts to embrace my true self, are a mere reflection of the potency of the ideals of personal growth and self-discovery that I embarked upon as a result of the pain and struggle I had to endure at a tender age. I am convinced that continuing education and support is what the world needs to bring out the best in our women and girls. With each passing day, I continue to deepen my pride in my Guyanese heritage, and this will continue to be my bedrock as an unrepentant advocate for the protection, education and the promotion of the wellbeing of my people, if only because fundamental human rights are not a privilege to employ at the bargaining table, but simply a birthright of all people.

With actions that are now intentional to the point of the calculating, I plan to continue to advocate for the preservation of the culture of the peoples of my country, Guyana, in a bid to shape the correct narrative about knowledge of my roots. Indeed, returning to my Guyanese roots after years of living in America has allowed me to rediscover those essential parts of my identify that are at the same time that faint echo in my heart that has made my life journey mature into a profound appreciation of the richness of my Guyanese culture, and the indomitable spirit of its people. I now appreciate the importance of preserving my family traditions, and armed with this new resolve, and newfound knowledge and understanding, I am renewed in my resolve to share my heritage with the world in my capacity as a Guyanese woman ambassador living in America.

13

Miss CARICOM

"The beauty of a woman is not in a facial mode but the true beauty in a woman is reflected in her soul. It is the caring that she lovingly gives the passion that she shows. The beauty of a woman grows with the passing years." - Audrey Hepburn

The joint establishment of the Miss CARICOM International Foundation, and Miss CARICOM International Beauty Pageant, was the culmination of my dreams for a wonderful and impactful initiative to celebrate the beauty, diversity, and culture of the peoples of the CARICOM region. Twenty countries make up the Caribbean Community (CARICOM), fifteen of which are full members, while five are Associate Members. The geographical boundaries of CARICOM stretch from The Bahamas in the north, southward to Guyana and Suriname, both on the north coast of the South American mainland. They also extend from Belize in the West on the Central American mainland to Barbados, the most easterly of the islands. Suriname defines the eastern boundary of the Community.

All CARICOM countries are classified as developing countries. They are all relatively small in terms of population and size, and diverse in terms of geography and population, culture and levels of economic and social development. The CARICOM countries share similarities and challenges. On the one hand, they are all in proximity to major markets in North and South America, and most countries have had to make the transition from agriculture or mining to a service-driven economy, especially tourism and financial services. On the other hand, they have to overcome the challenges of frequent natural disasters, in addition to small sizes with associated lack of economies of scale and vulnerability to external shocks. This organization of Caribbean countries and dependencies, originally established as the Caribbean Community and Commons Market in 1973 by the Treaty of Chaguaramas, replaced the former Caribbean Free Trade Association (CARIFTA), which had become effective in 1968. The treaty spurred the development of associate institutions, including the Caribbean Development Bank and the Organization of East Caribbean States, both of which promote economic growth and cooperation. Members include Barbados, Guyana, Jamaica, and Trinidad and Tobago are the founding members. The other countries that makeup CARICOM are Antigua and Barbuda, Belize, Dominica, Grenada, Montserrat, Saint Kitts and Nevis, Saint Lucia, and Saint Vincent the Grenadines, the Bahamas, Haiti, and Suriname.

CARICOM's main purposes are to promote economic integration and cooperation among its members, to ensure that the benefits of integration are equitably shared, and to coordinate foreign policy. Its major activities have centred on coordinating economic policies and development planning. It also devises and institutes special projects for the less-developed countries within its jurisdiction. In the late 1980s, CARICOM's heads of government declared their support for the creation of a regional common market, and, in 1990, members agreed to develop common protectionist policies for trade with countries outside the organization, though many members were slow to implement these and other decisions. In July 2001 the heads of government revised the Treaty of Chaguaramas, establishing the Caribbean Community and the CARICOM Single Market and Economy (CSME), which would harmonize economic policy and create a single currency.

During the course of my extensive research and planning for the Miss CARICOM initiative, I spoke with then secretary-general of CARICOM, Dr Edwin Carrington, and intimated him of my concept. He advised that this was a very good initiative, as CARICOM obviously needed more marketing and spotlight on the objectives of the community's programs, so that the world could become more aware of the critical issues facing the region. Naturally, I was very grateful for his valued input, as Dr Carrington had what might be accurately termed a bird's eye view of CARICOM as a whole. My extensive research covered existing beauty pageant formats, criteria, and successful execution within the CARICOM region. In the process, I successfully identified gaps in originality, and other unique aspects that I could infuse into my own concept, and which would adequately highlight the unique cultural heritage, diversity, and beauty of the region.

I developed a detailed business plan, including financial projections, marketing strategies, sponsorship opportunities, and a timeline for event execution, and incorporated everything into a Concept Paper. That was the proposal I was carrying all over the place when I first met Mr Danny Glover, and pointedly asked him to lend his name to the project, and become its patron, so that I could more effectively engage key potential stakeholders in the CARICOM region. I sent out my marketing information to the beauty, fashion, and tourism industries. I collaborated with modeling agencies, beauty brands, fashion designers, tourism boards, media outlets, and relevant cultural organizations. I forged partnerships to secure requisite support, resources, and expertise that aligned with the vision and objectives of Miss CARICOM International Foundation and the beauty pageant. My *Participant Recruitment and Selection Committee* developed a transparent and fair process for recruiting and selecting participants from CARICOM member countries. I considered criteria such as age limits, nationality requirements, talent or skill assessments, cultural knowledge, and a commitment to representing the region's values and heritage. I ensured diversity and inclusivity in participant selection to showcase the rich tapestry of the Caribbean's beauty. I also added a platform of presentation that allowed participants to showcase their speaking abilities.

I vigorously promoted the *Cultural Showcase and Event* activities that highlighted the unique traditions, music, dance, fashion, and cuisine of the CARICOM region. I organized pre-pageant events, workshops, and cultural exchanges to provide participants with opportunities to connect and learn from each other's cultures. I devoted particular attention to *Environmental and Social Responsibilities* throughout the pageant. I created opportunities for participants to engage in community service activities, environmental conservation efforts, and charitable initiatives that contributed positively to CARICOM member countries. To market and promote the region, I rotated the final crowing event amongst the different CARICOM countries, each year, in a bid to raise awareness about each member state of the CARICOM region, our foundation and the beauty pageant. We utilized various channels, such as social media, websites, press releases, while collaborating with influencers, and assiduously employing targeted advertising campaigns. For instance, when the pageant held in Montserrat, the objective was to help the people of Montserrat achieve the goal of *transit commerce,* so that the island could escape the clamor for its closure, as suggested even by Queen Elizabeth II of England. Miss CARICOM Beauty Pageant helped to drive commerce traffic to the island. The pageant demonstrated that the near-moribund island was still socially functional and economically viable. At that time, the Island needed to meet a certain economic quota within a stipulated period of time. The pageant enabled the struggling island to meet stringent requirements with respect to traffic of people and commerce.

Miss CARICOM International Beauty Pageant had a network that covered its activities on the island. That network was launched based exclusively on the activities surrounding the pageant. In effect, we saved the island of Montserrat from its untenable situation at that time. The beauty pageant was, and remains a consummately structured pageant designed to highlight, showcase, promote and preserve the culture of the peoples of the CARICOM region. Because of the attention we studiedly devoted to organizing and executing the beauty pageant, especially with regards to professionalism, we were able to orchestrate a well-organized production, including stage design, lighting, sound, and multimedia setups that reflect the vibrancy and spirit of the CARICOM region. Additionally, we studiously maintained fairness and transparency throughout the judging and scoring processes.

Our legacy, and our sustained engagement with the CARICOM region is to nurture the CARICOM beauty pageant beyond what its initial editions offered. This now includes offering mentorship opportunities, ambassadorships, and career development programs for participants. We maintain engagement with alumni, and leverage their experiences to continue to promote the beauty and culture of the CARICOM region. Our United Nations exposure and education has encouraged collaboration, not only with CARICOM Institutions, but also with other entities that can relate to the cultural disparities and issues that are eloquently addressed through the pageant and what it represents. Miss CARICOM Foundation is a cultural non-profit that is dedicated to preserving, showcasing and promoting culture worldwide. Our platform addresses gender issues, educational issues, and other such concerns that lie at the core of the United Nations Sustainable Development Goals for the marginalized regions and rural areas of the world. Our platform now allows our presence to be felt in countries outside of the CARICOM region, where we are exploring opportunities, and collaborating with institutions that share the concerns and views of the Miss CARICOM Foundation.

Suffice it to say that such partnerships have helped in raising the profile of both the foundation and the pageant, while strengthening our connection to the region's overall objectives and initiatives. The United Nations and its sustainable development goals, and Miss CARICOM's committed involvement with those goals keeps us under the obligation of continually evaluating and improving on our own policies, processes and procedures, especially with regards to the preservation of culture, educational initiatives, and heritage. We continue to assess the success of our involvement in communities, and focus on identifying areas for assistance in future projects. In the final analysis, the establishment of the Miss CARICOM International Foundation and the beauty pageant has allowed us to create an exciting opportunity to showcase and celebrate the unique beauty, diversity, education and culture of the CARICOM region, and even beyond. To the glory of God, we have created a platform that places premium value on cultural heritage, diversity and inclusivity, empowerment, education and the UN SDGs, while also allowing us to promote the Miss CARICOM International Beauty Pageant worldwide.

14

Family, Friends And Allies

"Family should be the place where you can be your most complete
self. Where you're accepted and appreciated, seen and valued,
even in moments of disagreement. It should be your soft place to
fall, the place where you're reminded that no matter what happens
to you, in the face of your deepest challenges, you are loved." -
Oprah Winfrey

The terms "friends," "allies," and "alliances" describe the different types of
relationships that individuals or entities can have with others, or with each
other. Friends are individuals who share a mutual bond and connection,
often based on personal affinity, trust, and emotional support. Friendship
is typically a voluntary relationship built on shared interests, values, or
experiences. Friends provide companionship, empathy, and often engage
in activities together for mutual enjoyment. Allies, on the other hand,
are individuals or groups who come together to support and advocate
for a common cause or goal. They collaborate and work collectively to
achieve shared objectives, often addressing social, political, or cultural issues.
Allies recognize the importance of solidarity, understanding, and support
for marginalized or disadvantaged communities. Allies may not have a
personal bond, yet join forces based on shared interests and values. Alliances,

at the end of the spectrum of human relationships, often refer to formal agreements or partnerships between individuals, organizations, or countries. These collaborations are typically strategic, establishing a set of objectives, agreements, and mutual commitments. Alliances can be formed for various purposes, including economic, political, security, or social reasons. They provide a structured framework for cooperation and collective action to achieve common goals.

On a more intimate level, family relationships describe the connection and bonds shared by individuals who are related either by blood, marriage, or adoption. It encompasses the mutual trust, love, support, and understanding that exist between family members. Family relationships can be between parents and children, siblings, extended family members, or even chosen family. Family relationships are very important. If the family is the fundamental unit block on which society, and humanity as a whole, is built, family relationships represent the sustained and interactive interconnectedness that glues members of a family to each other. Family can exist in many forms, and as a woman who has played the vital role of a single parent for many more years than I care to remember, there are some things I now know to be important, especially what it really means to have people who consider themselves your family, and the mutual love you can share with them for the overall wellbeing of everyone. Such bonds are important because family helps us get through the most difficult, if not often disastrous, times and share our joy at the best of times. That is also why, if only because of these shared times of agony and rejoicing, even those with whom we are not related by blood can sometimes represent the very best of family essence in our lives.

Family is important because they can offer support and security, coupled with unconditional love. They will always seek and bring out the best in you even if you cannot see it for yourself. Family is important because they will, for the most part, be the only ones who can really understand you and bring you back to a place of peace and harmony. Family is also very vital in guiding you down the path of morality, especially with regards to outside influences such as dealing with drugs, alcohol, peer pressure, or those negativities directed at you by others. Your family might not be able to shield you from everything, but they will be able to assist you through the hard times and give you the tools you need to diffuse awkward situations. Family will provide you with a home if you do not have one, and they will point you in the right direction so that you can get back on your feet. Although family will often tell you what you do not want to hear, the truth proverbially being a very bitter pill to swallow, almost invariably, they do so out of love, and to help you grow.

Another reason why family is so important is because they can teach us to know our family history, which can shape our personality into something positive and give us a sense of direction. Marcus Garvey, my Caribbean ancestor, once said, "A people without the knowledge of their past history, origin, and culture is like a tree without roots." I stress the importance of family for a very good reason. There are some people who are not blessed with two parents, while those that are blessed with two parents might not be that close to their parents, and are closer to their aunts, uncles, or grandparents. That being said, for the last six years, single-parent families have held a steady rate of 35% of total households in the United States. In 2016, that percentage totaled out to approximately 24 million children living with single parents in the United States, which is more than the population of Florida. According to the Kid's Data Center, in 2016, 32% of single parents were living in poverty compared to 7% of two-parent family homes. There is a clear understanding that growing up in destitute homes can present academic obstacles, reduced access to safe communities, quality enrichment activities, and can cause a heightened risk of physical, behavioral, and emotional issues. That is why I speak so emphatically on the significance of family. When family comes together, they can make the impossible become possible, and give hope to those that they love so dearly and give them a fighting chance in this life. Parents, both married and single, and elders must hold each other accountable because our children are worth all the trouble we take in raising them properly. As the saying goes, "One generation plants the trees and another gets the shade."

I hold the firm belief that families have sober responsibilities and obligations towards each other. Growing up with a grandmother, uncles and aunts in a household where cultural norms, family dynamics, and individual roles were monitored, organized and executed by my grandfather, William Subryan, adequate emotional support was always available to us all during both the good times and the challenging times. There were, indeed, many challenges, but my grandfather held us together, making sure that we had the basic food, shelter and health care that guaranteed our human dignity, no matter how basic and subsistent. His financial situation was quite poor, but his strict and structured guidance kept us balanced. I felt safe, protected and loved by a grandmother who would listen and understand, and offer encouragement and comfort. I was happy, and enjoyed having a family, although that period of my life did not last long, as I became disconnected from that structure at an early age. However, I continue to cling to those warm thoughts of family. I definitely found great comfort in the idea of having people I could trust and love unconditionally. Admittedly, issues will often arise, but the saying that blood is thicker than water remains quite valid in our lives. In my own case, the privilege of belonging to a close knit family did not last very long. The name Subryan was one I was given at birth. It was my mother's family name. As I recall, the only family environment I had as a child; the foundation of my childhood, is no more than a fleeting dream now, as my mother passed away in 2003, and with that sad milestone went any delusions I had about having a family called the Subryans. Interestingly, the time of my mother's passing coincided with my nascent rise to fame, so to speak. That was the era of my meeting the larger than life Hollywood movie star, Mr Danny Glover, the launch of my foundation, and the beginning of my wonderful relationship with the United Nation and its SDGs. So many events took place in my life within a year of my mother's passing.

As it happened, my Subryan family would all but turn their backs on me, possibly in the terribly misguided notion that I would never amount to much in life. They were terribly mistaken. Today, I have held over 200 social charity events. I have spoken at the United Nations on world issues on more that seven occasions. I have submitted several written statements to the United Nation on topics of global significance, ranging across poverty, gender equality, education, marginalized communities, and sundry other such concerns of the SDGs. I have received hundreds of honors, citations, proclamations and awards. I have been spotlighted on several TV and radio shows. I have been inducted into several Who's Who. Yet, despite all these, I have never received a congratulatory message or acknowledgement from a Subryan family member. No Subryan family member has deemed it fit to attended any of my events. Rather, I have been the hapless victim of vicious verbal attacks and threats from the Subryans. It is now my conviction that I have taken enough from then, and that I owe myself the resolve of not taking more. My shock at their attitude towards me can only be imagined. I left that family at a young age, and although it was a happy interlude in my young life, my most significant memories are those of grinding poverty in that household. In the event, I often wonder what and how much a little child could have taken from such a poor family. We slept on the floor with very few beddings. In fact, our so-called mattress and beddings were no more than old clothes that we simply spread on the ground. I have felt very hurt by the attacks from the only family I had known as a child. Not quite understand the rationale for the hostility, I reached out to the older Subryans, but no one responded to my offers at rapprochement. I finally became convinced me that their attitude was borne of pent up feelings of animosity towards me, and that they were all involved in a general conspiracy to alienate me.

Yet, I survived on my own. I educated myself. I fought for my place in the world. I never took anything from the Subryan family. I never visited any harm on the Subryan family. I always considered them my only family, but they never embraced me, and they never showed me compassion, love, care or concern in later years. They never visited me, my children or grandchildren. They never contributed anything positive to my wellbeing or my existence. They have refused to acknowledge me as family. They held many family events to which I was never invited. I was totally excommunicated by this family; the only family I could call my own. As soon as my grandfather and grandmother passed away, I was all but abandoned by the Subryan family.

I would be diagnosed with cancer for the second time, sometime in the summer of 2021. As would be expected, I had to endure a series of procedures, including a lumpectomy, radiation and chemotherapy, majorly during the Christmas holidays of 2021. Thanksgiving was my last holiday of that year before I commenced the regiment of dealing with my cancer. On that Thanksgiving Day of 2021, thirty five people came to celebrate with me. They came from all over the country; Texas, Las Vegas, Pennsylvania, Atlanta, name it. They all came to be with me in Queens, New York, to show support, solidarity, care, love and concern for me about the journey ahead of me. They called it a Thanksgiving Christmas, since they knew I would be in the throes of cancer management during the Christmas holidays. It was the most caring thing anyone had ever done for me. At that gathering were my three children, my grandchildren and friends. Not a single Subryan was present.

These 35 people were my real family, because what they did is what family do. Family show compassion, care, understanding and support. The event was organized by a lady named Ms Carol Kurka, a white woman who lives in Pennsylvania. The widow of a pastor. she is my family. The love and support that this woman shows me on daily basis is what family is supposed to do. She is more family to me than any blood family that I have. I use these pages to express an enormous depth of gratitude to this wonderful woman. I thank her from the bottom of my heart for all that she has done in supporting me. In 2001, my only daughter was diagnosed with postpartum depression, schizophrenia and bipolar disorder. That was another devastating period in my life. In the circumstances, i I was left to raise my daughter's three children all alone. My covenant helpers during that testing period of my life were Ms Louise Lucas and Ms Carol Kurka, whose joint kindness afforded me the relief of sending my grandsons to Pennsylvania to attend school. Sending them out of New York was the best decision I could possibly have made at that time, as they were being threatened by gang members in the community. To escape the trauma and deadly threats from the gangs, I had to ship them out of the area. Ms Carol offered to board them for me. So, I sent them away with a monthly financial support. Had it not been for Miss Carol's spiritual support, love and compassion this would not have been possible. The love, care, compassion, understanding and interest she invested in those boys while they were with her in Pennsylvania is all too evident in how they have turned out God-fearing and well-rounded young adults. This is what family does. With real family, blood is de-emphasized. It has nothing to do with blood, but everything to do with the love of God, and compassion for mankind.

I was tested to the limit of human endurance during my cancer journey. One of such tests came from a blood relative of mine, a niece who was spending her vacation at my house, and who ended up teaching me some very harsh and cruel lessons. I will attempt to abbreviate a long story. My niece summoned the police to my house a total of twelve times on false complaints against me. She took me to court, asking to be reinstated in my house. She lied to the police about being assaulted by me. To receive service from the city, she searched my house in my absence, and took away personal information and documents, including my personal journal. She read that journal, and shared all the information she could gather therein with her friends. She brought a man into my house, and attempted to force me to allow him live in my house. She attempted to kill me by giving me poison to drink in my medicine. She started a campaign of calumny against me, and spread patent untruths about me amongst my friends in a bid to cause disaffection between them and me. This young lady did many despicable things too numerous to mention in this short narrative. The lessons she taught me will last me through my entire lifetime. Finally, I had to take out an order of protection just to have my peace of mind, whilst yet in the midst of the trial of my chemotherapy treatment and radiation for breast cancer. At that time, the journey was one filled with rocks and boulders, not only in my cancer treatment, but from my torment by family members. Everyone knows how traumatic the journey of cancer can be. It is as physically challenging as it is both mentally and emotionally challenging. Having to deal with cancer, and with the lies, betrayal, deceit, corruption and wickedness of a so-called loved one is not an easy road to travel while battling cancer.

As I already mentioned, and at the risk of sounding like a broken record, my niece taught me the harshest lesson of my life, and one that will continue to reverberate in my consciousness as long as I live. It is with no small degree of pain that I will have to characterize my niece as an extremely dangerous person, filled with both deception and perfidy. As I write the pages of this book, I still have court appearances in which I'm a defendant with regards to the false accusations from her. I say all these, not necessarily to malign or vilify anyone, but merely to establish without equivocation that family is not necessarily defined by blood connection. Rather, in its truest essence, family is a good friend who is caring, concerned, loving and attentive. Such a friend can actually be all the family you will ever need. I can say in all truthfulness that even though the Subryans pushed me aside, and threw me under the bus, I have found real family in the affectionate arms of Louise Lucas and Carol Kurka. I am grateful, blessed and thankful to my Lord, Jesus Christ, for providing me these covenant helpers who have played a tremendous role in my life's journey. Thank you, Miss Carol Kurka. Thank you, Miss Louise Lucas.

Epilogue

What The Future Holds

"Perhaps the butterfly is proof that you can go through a great deal of darkness yet become something beautiful." - Unknown

If you are reading these; the closing words of my remarkable odyssey, it only means you have taken the trouble to journey with me through the pages of this book. I thank you for that. Accept my sincere gratitude for making my effort a worthwhile one. The road of life can be long, hard and arduous. It is harder still if there is no hand to hold as you trudge along, weary from the burden of it all. The effort of writing this book itself was a journey all by itself. In reading this book to the end, you were merely accompanying me on the journey. Thank you for holding my hand, even as I held your own hand, as we made the journey together.

The toughest part of overcoming the trials and tribulations of life is forgiving all those who have contributed, in one way or the other, to those harrowing experiences. Yet, if there is one final message I would like you to take from our joint journey in this book, it is that we must forgive all such persons, and then dare to set those vital boundaries that will eventually protect who we are becoming. Each and every day, we must meet the challenge of being better than we were yesterday. People will always be quick to judge you, especially when they don't know your story. That is why, anytime I remember all those who have terrorized me, especially in my childhood, I am humbled by the

158

grace of God upon my life.

As we part ways, I ask you to reflect on my story, and to remember that I endured unthinkable trauma and abuse at the hands of my paternal grandmother and so-called godmother. I ask you to remember that I suffered undeserved juvenile incarceration at the unholy behest of the same grandmother. I ask you to remember that I was subjected to emotional trauma by a mother, who lacking structure and function in her own life, was a mere victim of her own unfortunate circumstances as *a child herself, struggling to mother a child.* I ask you to remember that my childhood innocence was robbed, resulting in early teenage pregnancy, just like my own mother. I ask you to remember that I had to witness, first hand, the degrading treatment and humiliation of my mother at the hands of men of all shades of character. I urge you to remember how I had to endure the betrayal of so-called family, ranging from an absentee father to brother, niece, uncles and aunties.

Yet, I ask you to celebrate with me as you remember that, despite all the attempts of my guardians to truncate all my efforts to acquire an education, I managed to defy all the odds to become a very educated and informed individual. I urge you to remember that my education is so well-rounded that I have emerged a truly sophisticated woman for all seasons. I ask you to remember that, despite leaving my homeland of Guyana a near-fugitive, I would return to the same country years later to a hero's welcome, celebrated by the government and the people of Guyana. I ask you to remember that I eventually achieved my dream of establishing my own global non-profit, Miss CARICOM International Foundation, together with its accompanying appendage, Miss CARICOM International Beauty Pageant, now considered a globally acclaimed platform for the celebration of culture and beauty. I ask you to remember that I am now privileged to strut the corridors of the headquarters of the world's most influential global body, and rub shoulders with kings, queens, heads of states and governments, and ambassadors of the nations that constitute our global family.

I am now in a position to safely declare that the impact of my journey so far, and the profound lessons I have learnt on that remarkable journey, have fostered a deeper understanding of who I really am, and a further understanding of the true essence of who I will continue to remain in the years ahead. My authentic efforts to embrace my *true* self are a mere reflection of the potency of the ideals of education, personal growth and self-discovery that I embarked upon as a result of the early emotional trauma I had to endure at a tender age. Because of my own poignant experience, I am convinced that continuing education and wholesome support is what the world's women and girls need to bring out the best in them.

With regards to my native Guyana, and with each passing day, my pride in Guyanese heritage continues to deepen, and I have vowed that this will continue to be the foundation of my unrepentant advocacy for the protection, education and the promotion of the wellbeing of my people. This is because their fundamental rights as human beings is not a privilege that is supposed to be at the whims and caprices of the government, but simply their birthright. Therefore, based on actions that are now singularly intentional, it is my firm resolve to continue to advocate for the preservation of the culture of the peoples of my homeland, Guyana, in such a way as to influence the evolution of the correct narrative about the history and politics of Guyana, and the rest of the Caribbean. I am proud to declare that my Guyanese heritage, even after years of living in America, allows me to continue to rediscover that core part of my identify that, at the same time, has rendered my life journey an opportunity to attain a mature and profound appreciation of the richness of my Guyanese culture, and the irrepressible spirit of its people. I vow to make renewed effort to share my heritage with the world in my capacity as a Guyanese woman ambassador living in the United States.

My future is now inextricably tied to the future of the girl child. With abiding faith in the UN SDGs, I will continue to fight and advocate for the protection of the girl child; to educate that child for a much better future, and a much better life. My mission will continue to be support and protection for the world's children, all the way from being children to becoming adults, such that they can grow steadily, and in a normal progression, from being babies to being toddlers, to being young adults, to being adults, and finally, to being elderly citizens, in a healthy and humane social structure. This is process is a right, and not a privilege.

The title of this book was deliberately contrived. *I am the child of a child*. My mother gave birth to when she was barely thirteen. For me, this has become a very personal issue. Yet, as a compelling global issue, it has assumed a relevance in every cultural setting, and in every social setting in which children are giving birth to children. As a compelling personal crusade, I believe that a primary obligation of governments all over the world must be to offer unassailable protection for their citizens, especially those in the vulnerable age groups. As I mentioned previously, even though I survived, and my children survived, the world is replete countless many who are not that fortunate. I remain truly grateful for the privilege to be alive to tell the story of my life, and that is why I have committed to a mission in which I will work relentlessly towards a better world for the children of the world, so that our world can move farther and farther away from the tragedy of children having children without guidance, nurturing and protection.

With regards to my sustained engagement with the CARICOM region, I will continue to nurture the CARICOM beauty pageant beyond its original concept. In future, the pageant will be offering mentorship opportunities, ambassadorships, and career development programs for participants. I will also leverage the experiences of the alumni of the pageant in such a way that they can continue to promote the ideals of the beauty pageant itself, and the culture of the CARICOM region. Without doubt, my United Nations exposure has encouraged collaboration with CARICOM institutions and other entities that relate to the cultural disparities and issues that are addressed through the pageant and what it represents. As a cultural non-profit, Miss CARICOM Foundation will continue to preserve, showcase and promote the culture of the Caribbean Community. The foundation also addresses all the concerns that lie at the heart of the United Nations Sustainable Development Goals for the marginalized regions of the world.

It is noteworthy that the strategic partnership with the UN has not only helped in burnishing the profile and image of both the foundation and the pageant, but also strengthened my connection to the CARICOM region's overall objectives and initiatives. The UN and its sustainable development goals, and my committed involvement with those goals obligates me to continually evaluating and improving on my processes, especially as they relate to the preservation of culture and heritage. Naturally, this means that I am continually assessing the success of my involvement in communities, so that I can focus on identifying areas for assistance in future projects. My hearty conclusion is that the establishment and evolution of the Miss CARICOM International Foundation and the beauty pageant has accorded me an exciting opportunity to showcase and celebrate the unique beauty, diversity, and culture of the CARICOM region.

As I write the closing words of this book, I can only give God both glory and honor for allowing me to be a traveler on such a remarkable journey. I believe that I have successfully redefined the generational baton handed to me, and as I share my story with you, my sincere hope is that my saga of courage, perseverance and resilience will be of immense and everlasting benefit to you. I thank you, most sincerely, for keeping faith with me to read up to the final words of this book. As I take my leave of you, I invite you to tap into your soul's deepest desires, and should you find yourself short of your own expectations, set goals to achieve those ideals, and start to act to reinforce those goals.

Discover exactly what it is that you want from life, and act in accordance with the values and goals you have set for yourself. Yes, simply decide to continue to be the best version of yourself for the rest of your life. Indeed, my humble verdict is that, with unflinching faith in God, all things are possible for those for whom the word impossible has no place in the vocabulary. That is my sincere wish for you too. Please accept assurance of my love and affection always.

Monica Sanchez
Queens, New York
September 2023

Made in the USA
Middletown, DE
04 November 2023

41791096R00106